THE ROCK MONSTERS GUIDE TO GUITAR

BY DAVE LAZARUS

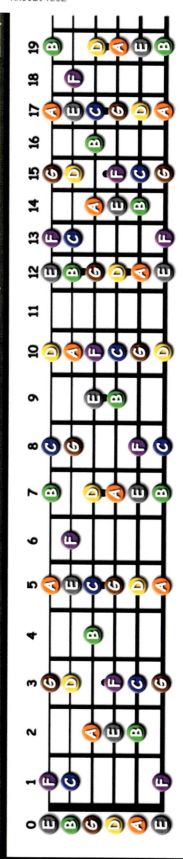

ILLUSTRATION CREDITS:

ROCK STARS ... MARC TILL SCHMID
MONSTERS ...   RICHARD CHAPLIN, JOVA GROF, PRZEMYSLAW DEDELIS, OMAIK NIEV, GEORGE ZAPATA

ALL IMAGES COPYRIGHT © 2013 – THE ROCK MONSTERS

ALL RIGHTS RESERVED

WWW.THEROCKMONSTERS.COM

COPYRIGHT© 2013

HOW TO USE THIS GUIDE:

THE FIRST PART OF THIS GUIDE COVERS THE CHORDS YOU NEED TO KNOW TO BEGIN DEVELOPING YOUR RHYTHM GUITAR SKILLS. START BY LEARNING TO PLAY POWER CHORDS AND BARRE CHORDS. YOU WILL BE ABLE TO PLAY TONS OF ROCK AND METAL SONGS WITH JUST THOSE CHORDS ALONE.
(CHORD CONSTRUCTION AND MORE COMPLEX CHORDS ARE COVERED NEAR THE END.)

THE SECOND PART COVERS THE SCALES YOU NEED TO KNOW TO DEVELOP YOUR LEAD GUITAR SKILLS. MEMORIZE THE 5 PATTERNS OF THE MINOR PENTATONIC SCALE AND HOW THEY FIT TOGETHER UP AND DOWN THE NECK. THEN GO STRAIGHT TO THE LICKS! PLAY THEM OVER AND OVER AS FAST AS YOU CAN. THIS WILL GET YOU STARTED RIPPING LEAD GUITAR!

LOOK AT THE BOOK WHILE YOU JAM ... OPEN THE BOOK TO THE SCALE YOU WANT TO PLAY ... PUT ON THE SONG YOU WANT TO PLAY TO ... AND JAM WHILE LOOKING AT THE SCALE YOU ARE PLAYING.
SEE THE ROOT NOTES, THE MINOR & MAJOR THIRDS, THE BLUE NOTES, AND ALL THE OTHER CHARACTERISTIC NOTES. IN TIME YOU WILL GET TO KNOW THESE NOTES BY "FEEL" AND WON'T NEED TO USE THE BOOK.

GO TO THE ROCK MONSTERS WEBSITE AND WATCH THE VIDEOS !!!

EVERYTHING IS EASY TO UNDERSTAND WHEN YOU MATCH THE VIDEOS ON THE WEBSITE TO THE DIAGRAMS IN THIS BOOK. IT'S ALL THERE TO HELP YOU.

PRACTICE — RULE OF THUMB SAYS THAT IT TAKES 10,000 HOURS OF PRACTICE TO MASTER A SKILL. THAT MEANS PLAYING GUITAR 4 HOURS A DAY FOR 7 YEARS. (ALL THE GREAT GUITAR PLAYERS IN THIS GUIDE PLAYED THAT MUCH, IF NOT MORE.) YOU MIGHT NOT BE ABLE TO PRACTICE THAT MUCH, BUT YOU STILL NEED TO PUT IN THE TIME IT TAKES IF YOU WANT TO BE A GOOD GUITAR PLAYER. THERE'S NO SHORT CUTS. PRACTICE EVERY DAY!!!

IT'S BETTER TO PLAY 30 MINUTES EVERY DAY THAN 3 HOURS ONE DAY.

PLAYING EVERY DAY MAKES YOU DEVELOP THE TOUGH, HARD CALLUSES YOU NEED ON THE TIPS OF YOUR FINGERS. THEN THE STRINGS WON'T HURT, YOU'LL BE ABLE TO PLAY WITH PROPER TECHNIQUE, GET A GOOD TONE, AND RIP!

ASK YOUR PARENTS TO READ THE "GUIDE FOR PARENTS" ON THE LAST PAGE. YOU WILL BE HAPPY YOU DID.

IT'S CALLED "PLAYING" GUITAR BECAUSE IT'S ALL ABOUT HAVING FUN!

WWW.THEROCKMONSTERS.COM
COPYRIGHT© 2013

THE ROCK MONSTERS GUIDE TO GUITAR

BY DAVE LAZARUS

CHORDS

- POWER CHORDS...7
- BARRE CHORDS...9
- MAJOR TRIADS...10
- MINOR TRIADS...11
- SUS CHORDS...52
- ADD9 CHORDS...53
- 7TH CHORDS...54
- 9TH CHORDS...56
- 11TH CHORDS...58
- 13TH CHORDS...59
- CHORDS COMPLETE...60

SCALES

- MINOR PENTATONIC...12
- MAJOR PENTATONIC...14
- LICKS ~ KEY OF A...18
- WITH PASSING TONES...26
- THE 7 MODES...36
- IONIAN MODE...37
- DORIAN MODE...38
- PHRYGIAN MODE...39
- LYDIAN MODE...40
- MIXOLYDIAN MODE...41
- AEOLIAN MODE...42
- LOCRIAN MODE...43
- HARMONIC MINOR...47

BIOS

- JIMI HENDRIX...4
- EDDIE VAN HALEN...6
- SLASH...8
- JIMMY PAGE...20
- ANGUS YOUNG...24
- ERIC CLAPTON...28
- JOE PERRY...30
- STEVIE RAY VAUGHAN...32
- TONY IOMMI...34
- RANDY RHOADS...46
- KIRK HAMMETT...48
- KEITH RICHARDS...50

EVERYTHING ELSE

- GETTING IN TUNE...5
- BENDING & VIBRATO...29
- ROCK RIFFS...31
- THE BLUES...33
- METAL...35
- METAL LICKS...49
- PICKUPS, AMPS, & FX...62
- CHANGING STRINGS...63
- ROCK HISTORY 101...64
- PERFORMANCE TIPS...65
- GUIDE FOR PARENTS...69

LET'S GET ROCKIN!

Jimi Hendrix

JAMES MARSHALL HENDRIX WAS BORN ON NOVEMBER 27, 1942 IN SEATTLE, WA.

WHEN JIMI WAS YOUNG HE USED TO SIT AT THE END OF HIS BED AND STRUM A BROOM LIKE HE WAS PLAYING A GUITAR. (1952) HIS FATHER FOUND AN OLD UKULELE WITH ONE STRING THAT HE GAVE TO JIMI. (1955)

WHEN JIMI WAS 15 HIS FATHER BOUGHT HIM AN ACOUSTIC GUITAR AND HE JOINED HIS FIRST BAND. (1958) WHEN JIMI WAS 16 HIS FATHER BOUGHT HIM HIS FIRST ELECTRIC GUITAR AND JIMI JOINED A BAND CALLED "THE ROCKING KINGS."

JIMI LEARNED TO PLAY BY WATCHING AND GETTING TIPS FROM MORE EXPERIENCED PLAYERS, BY PLAYING ALONG WITH HIS BLUES RECORDS, AND PRACTICING CONSTANTLY. (1959)

JIMI'S BIGGEST INFLUENCES WERE BLUESMEN LIKE MUDDY WATERS, BUDDY GUY, HOWLIN' WOLF, B.B. KING, AND ROBERT JOHNSON.

THE VOODOO CHILD

WHEN JIMI WAS 19 YEARS OLD HE LEFT HOME TO JOIN THE ARMY. WHILE STATIONED AT FORT CAMPBELL IN KENTUCKY, JIMI FORMED A BAND CALLED "THE KING CASUALS." (1961)

JIMI WAS A TERRIBLE SOLDIER AND WAS DISCHARGED FROM THE ARMY AFTER SERVING ONLY ONE YEAR. HE THEN BEGAN WORKING AS A SESSION GUITARIST UNDER THE NAME "JIMMY JAMES." BY THE TIME JIMI WAS 23 YEARS OLD HE HAD PLAYED AND TOURED WITH IKE & TINA TURNER, SAM COOKE, THE ISLEY BROTHERS, AND LITTLE RICHARD. (1963)

JIMI MOVED TO NEW YORK AND PLAYED THE SMALL CLUBS IN GREENWICH VILLAGE. (1965) WHEN HE WAS 24 YEARS OLD, JIMI MOVED TO LONDON TO FORM A NEW BAND. (1966)

JIMI WAS 24 YEARS OLD WHEN HE RECORDED HIS 1ST ALBUM, "ARE YOU EXPERIENCED," AND REVOLUTIONIZED THE WAY THE ELECTRIC GUITAR IS PLAYED FOREVER. (1967)

GETTING IN TUNE

THE FIRST THING YOU SHOULD DO WHENEVER YOU PICK UP THE GUITAR IS GET IN TUNE. IT CAN BE VERY DISCOURAGING TO PLAY AN OUT-OF-TUNE GUITAR.

1. BUY A $20 ELECTRONIC GUITAR TUNER AND USE IT.
HINT: SELECT THE BRIDGE PICKUP ON YOUR GUITAR. TURN THE VOLUME AND TONE KNOBS ALL THE WAY UP.

ALWAYS TUNE UP!
THIS MEANS THAT YOU LOOSEN THE STRING UNTIL IT'S BELOW THE DESIRED PITCH AND INCREASE THE TENSION OF THE STRING UNTIL IT REACHES THE RIGHT PITCH. IF YOU GO TOO FAR, LOOSEN THE STRING AND **TUNE UP** AGAIN.

... AND TUNING DOWN ...
MOST GUITAR MUSIC IS IN STANDARD TUNING. IN **STANDARD TUNING** YOUR STRINGS ARE TUNED:

E, A, D, G, B, E (LOW-TO-HIGH)

SOME GUITAR PLAYERS (JIMI HENDRIX, VAN HALEN, SRV, SLASH ...) TUNE ALL THE STRINGS DOWN A HALF-STEP TO **E FLAT** WHICH SOUNDS HEAVIER. BLACK SABBATH TUNE DOWN A STEP-AND-A-HALF TO **C SHARP** WHICH SOUNDS SUPER HEAVY!

ONCE YOU HAVE TUNED UP ALL SIX STRINGS, GO BACK AND CHECK THEM AGAIN AND MAKE MINOR ADJUSTMENTS. REMEMBER TO **TUNE UP** TO REACH THE CORRECT PITCH.

LEARN HOW TO TUNE USING HARMONICS ON THE 5TH AND 7TH FRETS. HINT: LISTEN FOR THE WAH-WAH-WAH TO BECOME A STEADY WAAAAHHHH.

IT'S ALL RIGHT IF IT TAKES A WHILE TO GET THE HANG OF TUNING YOUR GUITAR. WITH PRACTICE YOU'LL BE A PRO!

TUNE IT UP!

EDDIE VAN HALEN

EDWARD LODEWIJK VAN HALEN WAS BORN ON JANUARY 26, 1955 IN AMSTERDAM, HOLLAND.

WHEN HE WAS 5, EDDIE, AND HIS OLDER BROTHER, ALEX, STARTED TAKING CLASSICAL PIANO LESSONS. (1960) EDDIE DIDN'T READ MUSIC. HE LEARNED HOW TO PLAY PIECES BY MOZART, BACH, AND BEETHOVAN PERFECTLY BY EAR.

WHEN EDDIE WAS 7 YEARS OLD HIS FAMILY MOVED FROM HOLLAND TO THE UNITED STATES. (1962) EDDIE AND ALEX CONTINUED THEIR PIANO LESSONS. EDDIE WON 1ST PLACE THREE YEARS IN A ROW PLAYING THE PIANO IN TALENT CONTESTS IN LOS ANGELES. (1965)

AT FIRST EDDIE WANTED TO PLAY THE DRUMS. HE GOT A DRUM SET WHEN HE WAS 10 YEARS OLD AND GOT A PAPER ROUTE TO PAY FOR THEM. WHILE EDDIE WAS OUT DELIVERING PAPERS, ALEX WOULD PLAY EDDIE'S DRUMS. PRETTY SOON ALEX WAS BETTER THAN EDDIE AT THE DRUMS, SO EDDIE DECIDED TO SWITCH TO PLAYING THE GUITAR. (1966)

EDDIE GOT HIS FIRST ELECTRIC GUITAR WHEN HE WAS 12 YEARS OLD. (1967) HE WOULD SIT IN HIS ROOM "ALL DAY, EVERY DAY" PRACTICING PLAYING HIS GUITAR.

EDDIE'S BIGGEST INFLUENCE IS ERIC CLAPTON FROM WHEN ERIC WAS IN THE BAND "CREAM." EDDIE SAYS HE GOT THE IDEA FOR TAPPING WHILE WATCHING JIMMY PAGE PLAY THE GUITAR SOLO IN "HEARTBREAKER" AT A LED ZEPPELIN CONCERT. (1972)

EDDIE AND ALEX PLAYED IN BANDS TOGETHER ALL THROUGH HIGH SCHOOL. AFTER THEY GRADUATED THEY MET DAVID LEE ROTH AND MICHAEL ANTHONY AND TOGETHER THEY FORMED VAN HALEN. (1974) THEY PLAYED BACKYARD PARTIES, THE CLUBS ON THE SUNSET STRIP IN HOLLYWOOD, AND ANYWHERE ELSE THEY COULD GET A GIG. (1976)

EDDIE WAS 22 YEARS OLD WHEN VAN HALEN RECORDED THEIR FIRST ALBUM IN 1977.

SLASH

SAUL HUDSON, A.K.A. "SLASH," WAS BORN ON JULY 23, 1965 IN LONDON, ENGLAND.

SLASH MOVED FROM LONDON TO LOS ANGELES WHEN HE WAS 11 YEARS OLD. (1976) HE DIDN'T FIT IN WITH THE OTHER KIDS IN SOUTHERN CALIFORNIA BECAUSE OF HIS LONG HAIR, RIPPED JEANS, AND CONCERT T-SHIRTS THAT HE WORE EVEN BACK THEN.

WHEN SLASH WAS 12 YEARS OLD HE MET STEVEN ADLER IN JUNIOR HIGH SCHOOL. (1977) THEY DECIDED TO FORM A BAND AND SLASH STARTED LEARNING TO PLAY ON AN ACOUSTIC GUITAR HIS GRANDMOTHER GAVE HIM THAT ONLY HAD ONE STRING (LOW E).

WHEN SLASH WAS 14 HE HEARD THE AEROSMITH ALBUM "ROCKS" AND IT "CHANGED HIS LIFE."

SLASH WAS ALSO DEEPLY INFLUENCED BY LED ZEPPELIN, ERIC CLAPTON, JEFF BECK, THE ROLLING STONES, AND JIMI HENDRIX.

SLASH'S GRANDMOTHER GAVE HIM HIS 1ST ELECTRIC GUITAR, A LES PAUL COPY, WHEN HE WAS 15 YEARS OLD. (1980)

SLASH SAYS THAT WHEN HE WAS IN HIGH SCHOOL HE PLAYED HIS GUITAR 12 HOURS A DAY. HE WOULD SKIP CLASS AND SIT IN THE BLEACHERS AT HIS SCHOOL AND PLAY GUITAR. (1981)

WHEN SLASH WAS 18 HE FORMED THE BAND "ROAD CREW" WITH STEVEN ADLER ON DRUMS. (1983) DUFF MCKAGAN JOINED THE BAND FOR A SHORT TIME AFTER ANSWERING AN AD SLASH PLACED IN THE PAPER LOOKING FOR A BASS PLAYER.

WHEN SLASH WAS 20 HE AND STEVEN JOINED AXL ROSE, IZZY STRADLIN', AND DUFF IN GUNS N' ROSES. THEY PLAYED THE CLUBS IN HOLLYWOOD FOR THE NEXT TWO YEARS.

THE CAT IN THE HAT

SLASH WAS 22 WHEN GUNS N' ROSES RECORDED "APPETITE FOR DESTRUCTION." (1987)

BARRE CHORDS

BARRE CHORDS ARE MOVEABLE CHORD SHAPES THAT CAN BE PLAYED ANYWHERE ON THE NECK OF THE GUITAR.

PLAY 30 MINUTES EVERY DAY!

MAJOR BARRE CHORDS

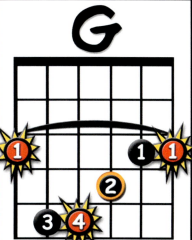

"E" SHAPE

6TH STRING ROOT

- 1ST FRET: F
- 3RD FRET: G
- 5TH FRET: A
- 7TH FRET: B
- 8TH FRET: C
- 10TH FRET: D
- 12TH FRET: E

MINOR BARRE CHORDS

6TH STRING ROOT

- 1ST FRET: Fm
- 3RD FRET: Gm
- 5TH FRET: Am
- 7TH FRET: Bm
- 8TH FRET: Cm
- 10TH FRET: Dm
- 12TH FRET: Em

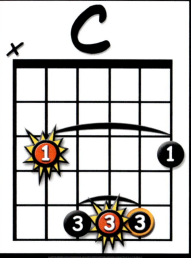

"A" SHAPE

5TH STRING ROOT

- 2ND FRET: B
- 3RD FRET: C
- 5TH FRET: D
- 7TH FRET: E
- 8TH FRET: F
- 10TH FRET: G
- 12TH FRET: A

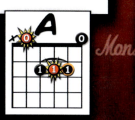

5TH STRING ROOT

- 2ND FRET: Bm
- 3RD FRET: Cm
- 5TH FRET: Dm
- 7TH FRET: Em
- 8TH FRET: Fm
- 10TH FRET: Gm
- 12TH FRET: Am

MAJOR TRIADS

ADD THE 3RD. MAJOR TRIADS ARE CONSTRUCTED FROM A ROOT (1ST), **NATURAL** 3RD, AND 5TH.

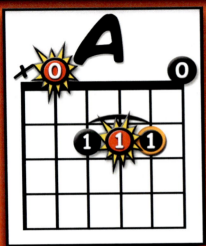
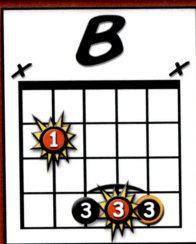
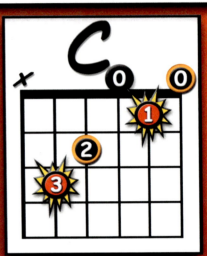
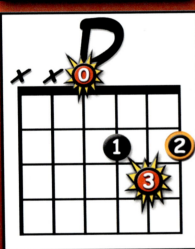
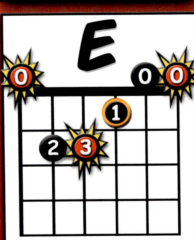
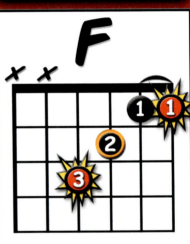

 ROOT NOTE

 MAJOR 3RD

DO NOT PLAY THE STRINGS MARKED WITH AN "X." THE STRINGS MARKED WITH AN "O" ARE PLAYED "OPEN."

TRIADS ARE CREATED BY TAKING EVERY THIRD NOTE FROM THE MAJOR SCALE. FOR INSTANCE, TAKING THIRDS FROM C WE GET C, E, AND G, WHICH MAKES A "C" CHORD.

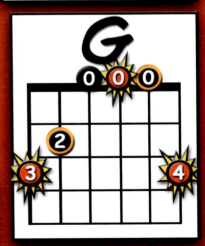

MINOR TRIADS

ADD THE MINOR 3RD. MINOR TRIADS ARE CONSTRUCTED FROM A ROOT (1ST), FLATTED 3RD, AND 5TH.

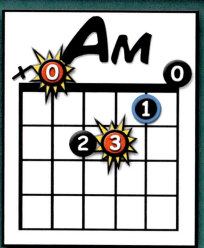
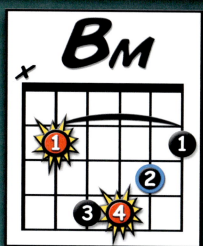

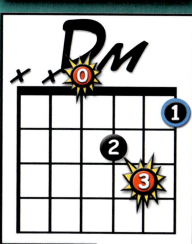
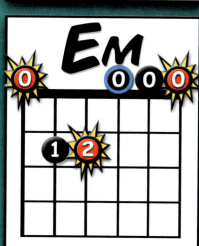
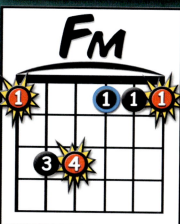

...THE SADDEST OF ALL CHORDS.

 MINOR 3RD
 5TH

STRUMMING ~ RELAX YOUR WRIST. STRUM WITH YOUR WRIST NOT YOUR ARM. FEEL THE RHYTHM. **TAP YOUR FOOT TO KEEP TIME.**

HOLD YOUR PICK FIRMLY BETWEEN YOUR THUMB AND INDEX FINGER. ONLY THE TIP OF THE PICK SHOULD BE STICKING OUT.

STRUM ONLY 2 OR 3 STRINGS AT A TIME ON AN ELECTRIC GUITAR WITH DISTORTION. ON AN ACOUSTIC GUITAR, STRUM ALL THE STRINGS EXCEPT THE ONES WITH THE "X."

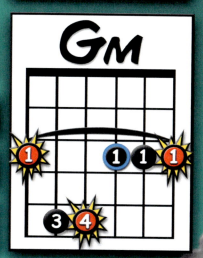

THE MINOR PENTATONIC SCALE

THE MINOR PENTATONIC SCALE SOUNDS "TOUGH AND MEAN" ~ "DARK AND SAD."

PATTERN 1

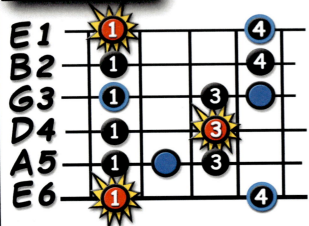

6TH STRING ROOT

PATTERN 2

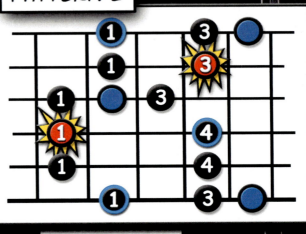

4TH STRING ROOT

THE ROOT NOTE (1ST) = RESOLUTION

HOLD THIS NOTE. IT FEELS GOOD TO REST HERE. THIS NOTE IS *THE KEY* YOU'RE PLAYING THE SCALE IN.

THE MINOR 3RD

IF THE 3RD IS FLAT, THE SCALE IS MINOR.

PLAY THIS NOTE TO EMPHASIZE THE *MINOR TONALITY*. THIS IS WHAT MAKES IT "SAD."

THE MINOR PENTATONIC SCALE IS THE MOST COMMONLY USED SCALE IN ROCK MUSIC — IT IS EASY TO LEARN, EASY TO PLAY, AND SOUNDS GOOD OVER MANY ROCK CHORD PROGRESSIONS.

THE MINOR PENTATONIC IS A *SIMPLIFIED* VERSION OF THE *AEOLIAN MODE* (PG. 42).

THE MINOR AND MAJOR PENTATONIC SCALES HAVE THE SAME 5 FINGERING PATTERNS. TO MOVE FROM THE MINOR PENTATONIC TO THE MAJOR PENTATONIC, SHIFT THE PATTERNS DOWN < 3 FRETS ... (SEE PAGE 14 FOR MORE INFO ON THE MAJOR PENTATONIC.)

FRETTING HAND – TOUCH THE STRINGS WITH JUST THE TIPS OF YOUR FINGERS. (DON'T LET YOUR FINGERS COLLAPSE.) YOU DON'T NEED TO PRESS VERY HARD. USE A LIGHT TOUCH WITH YOUR FRETTING HAND.

PICKING HAND – HOLD YOUR PICK FIRMLY. USE ALTERNATE PICKING (DOWN/UP/DOWN/UP...) FOCUS ON DEVELOPING SPEED AND PRECISION WITH YOUR PICKING HAND. HERE YOU CAN USE A HEAVY HAND. **DIG IN TO THOSE STRINGS!!!**

NOTICE HOW THE PATTERNS CONNECT TO EACH OTHER AS YOU MOVE UP AND DOWN THE NECK.

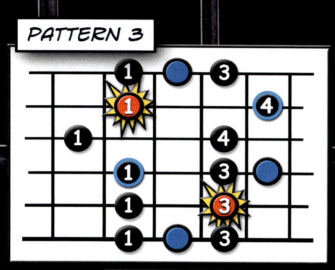

PATTERN 3
2ND STRING ROOT

PATTERN 4
5TH STRING ROOT

PATTERN 5
3RD STRING ROOT

THE "BLUE NOTE" = TENSION A.K.A. THE "WORRIED NOTE." ADDING THIS NOTE (THE FLATTED 5TH) TO THE MINOR PENTATONIC SCALE CREATES **THE BLUES SCALE**. BEND UP TO THIS NOTE AND HOLD IT. FEEL HOW IT CREATES TENSION.

TO FIGURE OUT THE **ROOT NOTE** – PLAY THE FIRST AND LAST CHORDS OF THE SONG. (TYPICALLY THEY ARE THE SAME.) THAT CHORD IS **THE "KEY"** OF THE SONG. USE THE 1ST NOTE OF THAT CHORD AS YOUR ROOT.

6TH STRING ROOT
- 1ST FRET: F
- 3RD FRET: G
- 5TH FRET: A
- 7TH FRET: B
- 8TH FRET: C
- 10TH FRET: D
- 12TH FRET: E

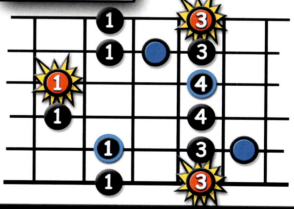

INTERVAL FORMULA:
ROOT b3 4 5 b7 OCTAVE
  W+H W W W+H W

GO TO THEROCKMONSTERS.COM FOR VIDEO EXAMPLES.

The Major Pentatonic Scale

The major pentatonic scale sounds **"cheerful"** but can also be **"wistful."**

Pattern 1

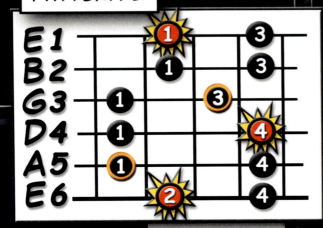

6th String Root

Pattern 2

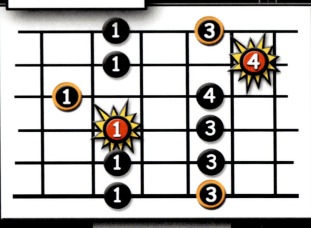

4th String Root

The Root Note (1st) = Resolution

Hold this note. It feels good to rest here. This note is **the key** you're playing the scale in.

The Major 3rd

If the 3rd is "natural" (not sharp or flat) the scale is major.

Play this note to emphasize **the major tonality**. This is what makes it "happy."

Jimi Hendrix, Jimmy Page, Eric Clapton, Slash,... are masters at alternating between the major and minor pentatonic scales to play interesting solos.

The major and minor pentatonic scales share the same 5 fingering patterns. Pattern 1 of the major pentatonic is the same as pattern 2 of the minor pentatonic. To move from the major pentatonic to the minor pentatonic, shift the patterns up > 3 frets ... (See page 12 for more info on the minor pentatonic.)

GO TO WWW.THEROCKMONSTERS.COM FOR VIDEO EXAMPLES.

"PENTA" MEANS FIVE IN GREEK. "TONIC" MEANS NOTE. A "PENTATONIC" SCALE IS A FIVE NOTE (TONE) SCALE.

A DIATONIC SCALE IS A SEVEN NOTE SCALE. SEE THE SECTION ON THE MODES (PAGE 36) FOR MORE INFO ON THE DIATONIC SCALES.

NOTICE HOW THE PATTERNS CONNECT TO EACH OTHER AS YOU MOVE UP AND DOWN THE NECK.

PATTERN 3

2ND STRING ROOT

PATTERN 4

5TH STRING ROOT

PATTERN 5

3RD STRING ROOT

THE MAJOR PENTATONIC IS A **SIMPLIFIED** VERSION OF THE **IONIAN MODE** (SEE PAGE 37).

---THE MAJOR SCALE---
"BRIGHT" "VIBRANT" "HAPPY"

IF YOU ARE PLAYING A SONG IN A MAJOR KEY AND WANT THE SOLO TO SOUND "HOT" AND "SWEET", THEN USE THE MAJOR PENTATONIC SCALE.

THE MAJOR PENTATONIC SCALE SOUNDS GREAT OVER UP-BEAT ROCK SONGS, COUNTRY SONGS, R&B AND SOUL SONGS, REGGAE,... LISTEN TO HOW LYNYRD SKYNYRD USES IT TO SOUND WISTFUL IN "TUESDAY'S GONE."

INTERVAL FORMULA:
ROOT 2 3   5 6   OCTAVE
 W   W W+H W W+H

15

Major Pentatonic Connected

HOW TO CONNECT THE PATTERNS AND MOVE DIAGONALLY UP AND DOWN THE NECK OF THE GUITAR.

6TH STRING ROOT ~ CONNECTING MAJOR PENTATONIC PATTERNS: 1, 2, 3, & 4.

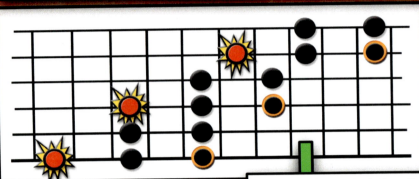

COUNT UP 1,2,3,1,2... DOWN 1,2,1,2,3...

G MAJOR PENTATONIC

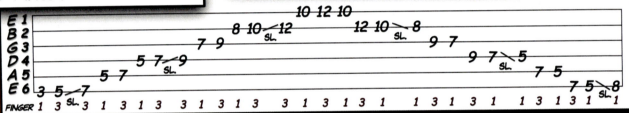

5TH STRING ROOT ~ CONNECTING MAJOR PENTATONIC PATTERNS: 4, 5, 1, & 2.

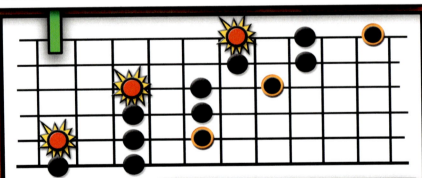

COUNT UP 1,2,1,2,3... DOWN 1,2,3,1,2...

G MAJOR PENTATONIC

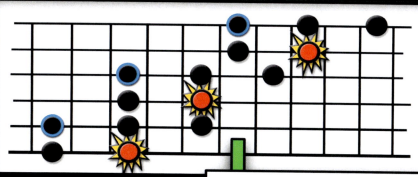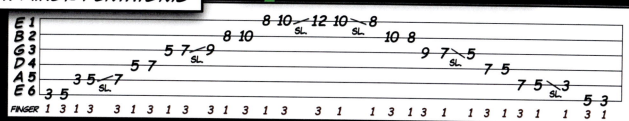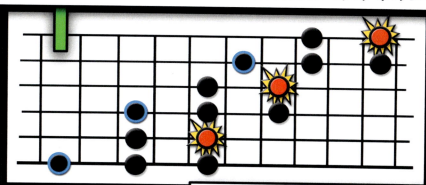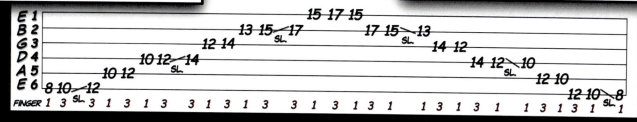

Minor Pentatonic Licks
Pattern 1 – Key of A

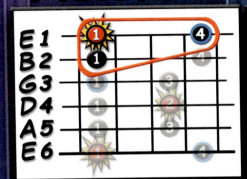 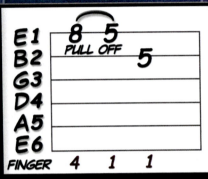

HOLD DOWN THE 1ST AND 2ND STRING WITH YOUR 1ST FINGER. PULL OFF WITH YOUR PINKIE.

HERE YOU PULL OFF FROM THE MINOR 3RD TO THE ROOT NOTE. THE JIMMY PAGE LICK.

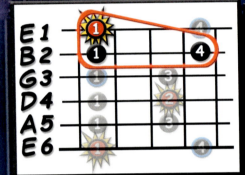 

HOLD DOWN THE 1ST AND 2ND STRING WITH YOUR 1ST FINGER. **HAMMER-ON** WITH YOUR PINKIE.

WHENEVER YOU INCLUDE THE ROOT NOTE YOU ESTABLISH "HOME BASE." WHENEVER YOU INCLUDE THE FLATTED 3RD YOU EMPHASIZE THE MINOR TONALITY. ("SAD")

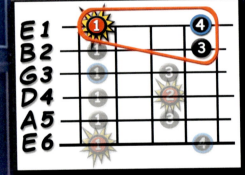 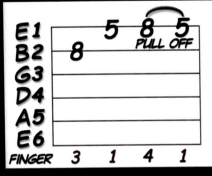

HOLD DOWN THE 1ST STRING WITH YOUR 1ST FINGER. **SHIFT YOUR 3RD FINGER OVER.** AFTER YOU PLAY THE 2ND STRING, LIFT YOUR 3RD FINGER SO THE PINKIE CAN GET IN THERE. PULL OFF WITH YOUR PINKIE.

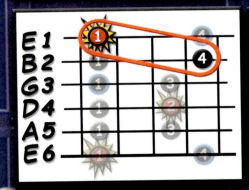 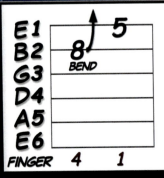

THIS IS CALLED A **UNISON BEND** – WHERE YOU BEND THE LOWER NOTE UP TO MATCH THE PITCH OF THE HIGHER NOTE. MAKE SURE YOUR INTONATION (PITCH) WITH THE BEND IS ACCURATE. THE NOTES SHOULD NOT "WOBBLE."

WHEN YOU PLAY THE MINOR AND MAJOR PENTATONIC SCALES THE NOTES LINE UP IN REOCCURING SHAPES. DEVELOP YOUR COORDINATION PLAYING LICKS WITH THESE 2, 3, AND 4 NOTE GROUPINGS.

GO TO WWW.THEROCKMONSTERS.COM FOR VIDEO EXAMPLES.

REPEAT EACH LICK OVER & OVER AS FAST AS YOU CAN!

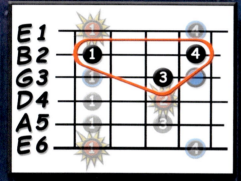
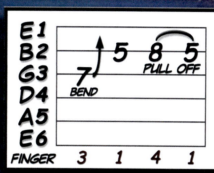

THE "CHUCK BERRY" LICK

ANOTHER UNISON BEND - BEND THE 3RD STRING UP A WHOLE STEP TO MATCH THE PITCH OF THE NOTE ON THE 2ND STRING. BE SURE TO REINFORCE THE BEND WITH YOUR 2ND FINGER.

SEE PAGE 29 FOR MORE INFO ON BENDING STRINGS.

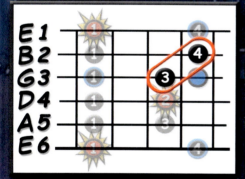
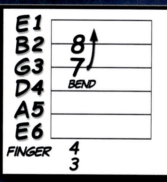

ONCE YOU GET TO THE TOP OF THE BEND, GENTLY **RELEASE THE PRESSURE ON THE STRING AND LET IT DOWN EASY** SO YOU ARE READY TO QUICKLY BEND IT UP AGAIN.

THIS IS CALLED AN **OBLIQUE BEND** - BE SURE TO REINFORCE THE BEND WITH YOUR 2ND AND 1ST FINGERS. KEEP YOUR PINKIE STILL. DON'T BEND THE 2ND STRING. HOLD IT. **MAKE IT SCREAM!** TRY IT WITH YOUR WAH PEDAL.

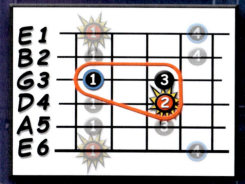
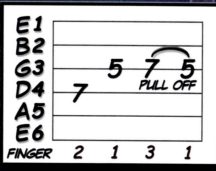

HOLD DOWN THE 3RD STRING WITH YOUR 1ST FINGER. SHIFT YOUR 2ND FINGER OVER. AFTER YOU PLAY THE 4TH STRING, LIFT YOUR 2ND FINGER SO THE 3RD FINGER CAN GET IN THERE. PULL OFF WITH YOUR 3RD FINGER.

19

JIMMY PAGE

JAMES PATRICK PAGE WAS BORN ON JANUARY 9, 1944 IN LONDON, ENGLAND.

WHEN JIMMY WAS 8 YEARS OLD HIS FAMILY MOVED TO A NEW HOUSE AND HE FOUND AN OLD ACOUSTIC GUITAR THAT HAD BEEN LEFT BEHIND BY THE PEOPLE THAT HAD LIVED THERE BEFORE.

WHEN JIMMY WAS 12 YEARS OLD HE WAS INSPIRED TO START PLAYING GUITAR AFTER HEARING THE ELVIS PRESLEY SONG "BABY, LET'S PLAY HOUSE." (1956)

JIMMY TOOK A FEW GUITAR LESSONS BUT MOSTLY TAUGHT HIMSELF BY PLAYING ALONG WITH HIS ROCK N' ROLL AND BLUES RECORDS FROM AMERICA.

WHEN JIMMY WAS 13 HE APPEARED ON TV PLAYING IN A SKIFFLE GROUP. SKIFFLE WAS AN ENGLISH VERSION OF AMERICAN ROCK N' ROLL. (1957)

JIMMY GOT HIS FIRST ELECTRIC GUITAR, A FUTURAMA "GRAZIOSO," WHEN HE WAS 15 YEARS OLD. (1959)

WHEN JIMMY WAS 16 HE WAS ASKED TO JOIN NEIL CHRISTIAN'S BAND "THE CRUSADERS." (1960) JIMMY TOURED WITH THEM FOR ABOUT TWO YEARS AND PLAYED ON SEVERAL OF THEIR RECORDS WHEN HE WAS 18.

THE WIZARD

WHEN JIMMY WAS 19, 20, AND 21 YEARS OLD HE WORKED AS A SESSION MUSICIAN IN LONDON'S RECORDING STUDIOS. (1963-1965) HE PLAYED GUITAR ON 100'S OF SONGS RECORDED DURING THAT TIME.

WHEN JIMMY WAS 22 HE WAS ASKED TO JOIN THE YARDBIRDS. (1966) THE YARDBIRDS ALREADY HAD HIT RECORDS AND WERE VERY POPULAR. JIMMY TOURED WITH THE YARDBIRDS FOR TWO YEARS AND DEVELOPED MOST OF THE SONGS HE WOULD LATER RECORD ON THE FIRST LED ZEPPELIN ALBUM.

JIMMY WAS 25 YEARS OLD WHEN HE RECORDED THE FIRST LED ZEPPELIN ALBUM. (1969)

MINOR PENTATONIC LICKS
PATTERN 2 – KEY OF A — ZIG ZAG

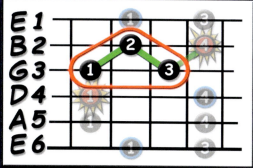
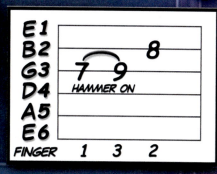

PATTERN 2 HAS A "ZIG-ZAG" SHAPE ON THE 2ND AND 3RD STRINGS. THIS NOTE GROUPING CREATES FUN, EASY TO PLAY "TRIANGLE LICKS." THIS LICK IS A GREAT WAY TO TRANSITION BETWEEN PATTERN 1 AND PATTERN 2.

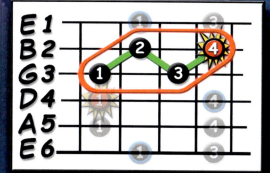
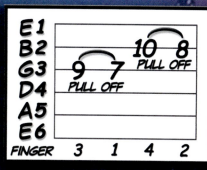

HERE IS THE 4 NOTE ZIG-ZAG GROUPING. HOLD DOWN THE 2ND AND 3RD STRINGS WITH YOUR 1ST AND 2ND FINGERS. IF YOU'RE JUST GETTING STARTED THIS ONE MIGHT BE A LITTLE TRICKY. BE PATIENT AND TAKE TIME TO DEVELOP YOUR COORDINATION.

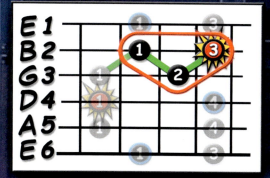
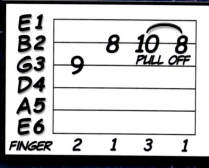

"TRIANGLE LICK" #2 HERE YOU PULL-OFF FROM THE ROOT NOTE TO THE FLATTED 7TH.

REPEAT EACH LICK OVER & OVER AS FAST AS YOU CAN!

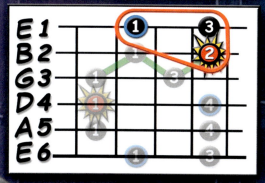
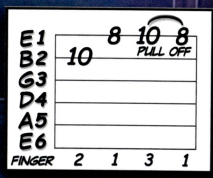

SHIFT YOUR 2ND FINGER OVER. AFTER YOU PLAY THE 2ND STRING, LIFT YOUR 2ND FINGER SO THE 3RD FINGER CAN GET IN THERE.

MINOR PENTATONIC LICKS

PATTERN 3 – KEY OF A

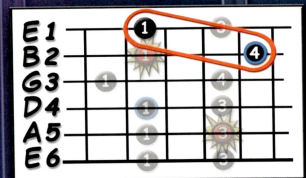

UNISON BEND. KEEP YOUR 1ST FINGER STILL. DON'T BEND THE 1ST STRING. REINFORCE THE BEND WITH YOUR 3RD AND 2ND FINGERS. MAKE SURE YOUR INTONATION WITH THE BEND IS CORRECT.

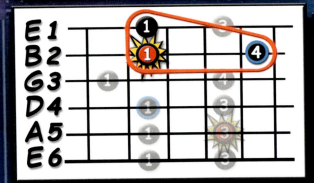
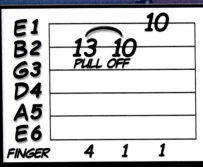

THESE SAME SHAPES ARE ALSO FOUND IN PATTERN 1. HEAR HOW THEY HAVE A DIFFERENT EFFECT WHEN YOU PLAY THEM IN PATTERN 3 BECAUSE OF WHERE THE ROOT NOTE AND MINOR 3RD FALLS.

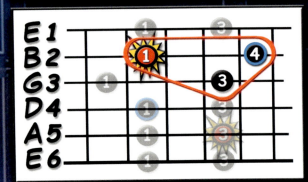
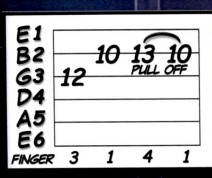

AGAIN, THE ROOT NOTE ESTABLISHES "HOME BASE." THE FLAT 3RD EMPHASIZES THE MINOR TONALITY.

REPEAT EACH LICK OVER & OVER AS FAST AS YOU CAN!

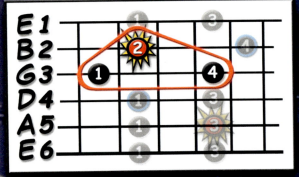
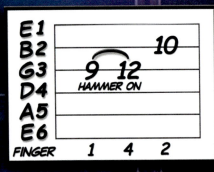

THIS SHAPE ALSO OCCURS IN PATTERN 5. THIS TIME USE HAMMER-ONS.

PLAY LICKS IN ONE PATTERN AND THEN QUICKLY MOVE TO ANOTHER PATTERN AND PLAY LICKS FROM THERE. KEEP MOVING. SEE HOW TO MOVE DIAGONALLY FROM PATTERN TO PATTERN IN THE "PENTATONIC SCALES CONNECTED" SECTIONS ON PAGES 16 AND 17.

PATTERN 4 — KEY OF A ZIG ZAG

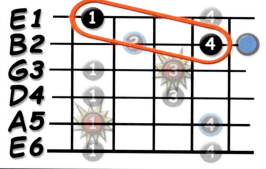
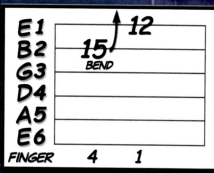

UNISON BEND.
BEND THE 2ND STRING UP A WHOLE STEP TO MATCH THE PITCH OF THE NOTE ON THE 1ST STRING. REINFORCE THE BEND WITH YOUR 3RD AND 2ND FINGERS.

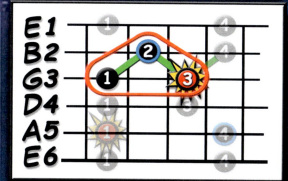
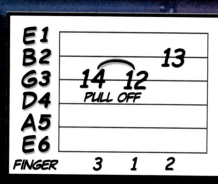

PATTERN 4 HAS THE ZIG-ZAG SHAPE ON THE 2ND AND 3RD STRINGS LIKE PATTERN 2. IN PATTERN 4 THE TRIANGLE LICKS INCLUDE THE ROOT NOTE AND THE MINOR 3RD MAKING THEM VERY EFFECTIVE.

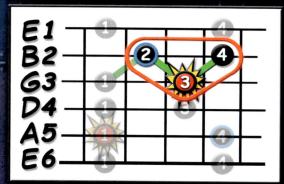
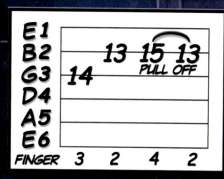

ZIG-ZAG SHAPE CONTINUED......
THIS TRIANGLE LICK ALSO INCLUDES THE ROOT NOTE AND THE MINOR 3RD, ESTABLISHING HOME BASE AND THE MINOR TONALITY.

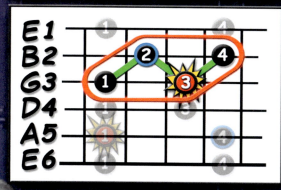
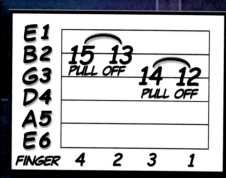

THIS LICK IS TOUGH. YOU GET EXTRA CREDIT IF YOU CAN PULL THIS ONE OFF. IT TAKES TIME. BE PATIENT AND KEEP PRACTICING.

ANGUS YOUNG

ANGUS MCKINNON YOUNG WAS BORN ON MARCH 31, 1955 IN GLASGOW, SCOTLAND.

ANGUS STARTED PLAYING GUITAR WHEN HE WAS 5 YEARS OLD. ONE OF HIS FRIENDS HAD A GUITAR THAT HE PLAYED WHENEVER HE WENT TO HIS FRIEND'S HOUSE. (1960)

WHEN ANGUS WAS 8 YEARS OLD HIS FAMILY MOVED TO SYDNEY, AUSTRALIA. (1963)

IN AUSTRALIA, ANGUS' OLDER BROTHER, GEORGE, FORMED A BAND CALLED "THE EASYBEATS." WHEN ANGUS WAS 11 THE EASYBEATS HAD A WORLDWIDE HIT WITH THE SONG, "FRIDAY ON MY MIND." (1966)

INSPIRED BY THEIR OLDER BROTHER'S SUCCESS, ANGUS AND HIS OLDER BROTHER, MALCOLM, BEGAN TO SERIOUSLY LEARN TO PLAY GUITAR.

AT FIRST ANGUS PLAYED MALCOLM'S GUITAR. FINALLY HIS MOTHER BOUGHT HIM A CHEAP ACOUSTIC GUITAR. ANGUS WAS 15 WHEN HE GOT HIS FIRST GIBSON SG. (1970)

WHEN HE WAS A TEENAGER ANGUS CONSTANTLY PRACTICED PLAYING THE GUITAR. AFTER SCHOOL HE DIDN'T EVEN TAKE TIME TO GET OUT OF HIS SCHOOL UNIFORM BEFORE HE PICKED UP HIS GUITAR.

THE LITTLE DEVIL

ANGUS' BIGGEST INFLUENCES ARE MUDDY WATERS, CHUCK BERRY, THE ROLLING STONES, AND THE WHO.

ANGUS WAS 18 YEARS OLD AND MALCOLM WAS 20 WHEN THEY FORMED AC/DC WITH ANGUS PLAYING LEAD GUITAR AND MALCOLM PLAYING RHYTHM GUITAR. (1973)

ANGUS WAS 19 WHEN AC/DC RECORDED THEIR FIRST ALBUM, "HIGH VOLTAGE" IN 1975.

Minor Pentatonic Licks
Pattern 5 – Key of A

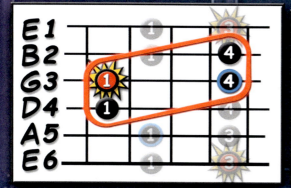

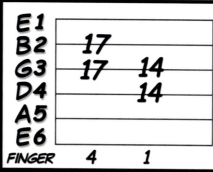

DOUBLE STOPS THICKEN AND ADD POWER TO YOUR SOUND. VERY CHUCK BERRY. TRY PLAYING LICKS FROM THE OTHER PATTERNS USING DOUBLE-STOPS.

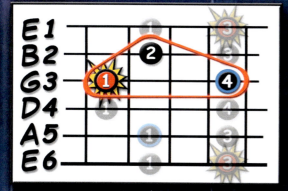

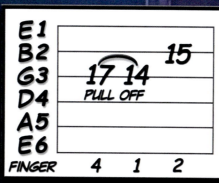

YOU FIND THE SAME SHAPE IN PATTERN 3. YOU GOTTA WORK YOUR PINKIE. USE A HAMMER-ON TO REVERSE IT.

THIS IS TO GET YOU STARTED JAMMING NOW! HOW MANY TIMES YOU REPEAT THE LICKS AND HOW YOU STRING THEM TOGETHER IS UP TO YOU. THAT'S YOUR STYLE.

AFTER YOU GET THE HANG OF THESE THREE NOTE GROUPINGS SOON YOU WILL START TO THINK IN TERMS OF FOUR NOTE GROUPINGS, AND FIVE NOTE GROUPINGS... WHEN YOU START PLAYING IN THE MODES (SEE PAGE 36) THEN YOU START SEEING SIX NOTE GROUPINGS AND THE POSSIBILITIES FOR LICKS GROWS EXPONENTIALLY.

* **THE MAJOR PENTATONIC HAS THE SAME SHAPES AND LICKS.** SHIFT THE PATTERNS DOWN < 3 FRETS TO PLAY THE MAJOR PENTATONIC IN THE SAME KEY. THE SCALES SOUND DIFFERENT BECAUSE THE ROOT NOTES ARE DIFFERENT.

** PAY SPECIAL ATTENTION TO YOUR **PICKING HAND.** THAT IS WHERE YOUR RHYTHM COMES FROM. DEVELOP YOUR TIMING AND ATTACK WITH YOUR PICKING HAND.

*** THESE EXAMPLES ARE IN THE KEY OF A. IT'S A VERY COMMON KEY AND YOU ARE ABLE TO CLIMB UP THE NECK AND PUT THE PATTERNS TOGETHER UNINTERRUPTED. IF IT IS DIFFICULT TO PLAY LICKS IN ANY PATTERN, CHANGE THE KEY AND PRACTICE THE LICKS WHERE IT IS EASIER. AROUND THE 12TH FRET OF THE GUITAR IS USUALLY THE EASIEST PLACE TO BEND THE STRINGS.

PENTATONIC SCALES WITH PASSING TONES

	PATTERN 1	PATTERN 2
MINOR PENTATONIC WITH AEOLIAN ○ PASSING TONES — THE MINOR SCALE	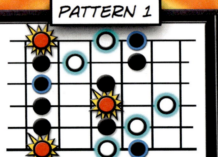	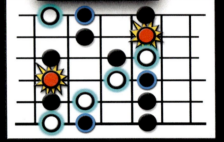
MINOR PENTATONIC WITH DORIAN ○ PASSING TONES  THE DIFFERENCE BETWEEN THE DORIAN AND THE AEOLIAN IS THE DORIAN HAS A NATURAL 6TH.	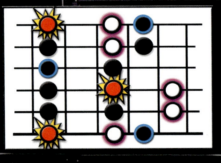	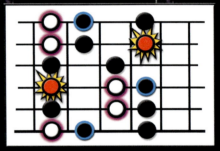
MINOR PENTATONIC WITH PHRYGIAN ○ PASSING TONES  THE DIFFERENCE BETWEEN THE PHRYGIAN AND THE AEOLIAN IS THE PHRYGIAN HAS A FLATTED 2ND.	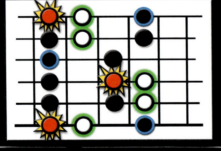	
MAJOR PENTATONIC WITH MIXOLYDIAN ○ PASSING TONES   MAJOR 3RD ○	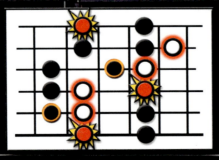	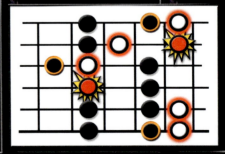

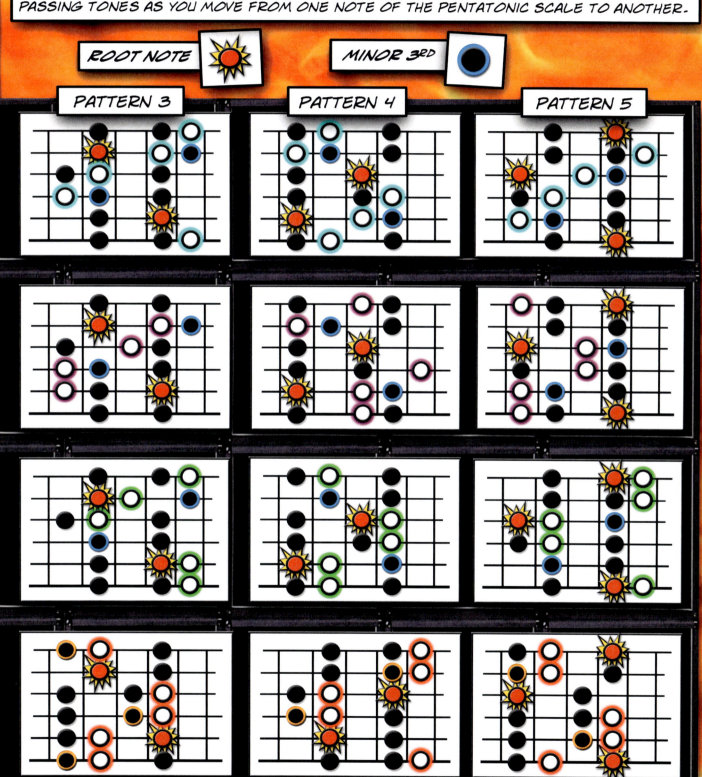

ERIC CLAPTON

ERIC PATRICK CLAPTON WAS BORN ON MARCH 30, 1945 IN RIPLEY, SURREY, ENGLAND.

MUSIC WAS ALWAYS A BIG PART OF ERIC'S LIFE. HIS GRANDMOTHER PLAYED PIANO EVERY AFTERNOON TO TAKE A BREAK AND HIS FAMILY LISTENED TO MUSIC ON THE RADIO ALL THE TIME.

SLOWHAND

ON HIS 13TH BIRTHDAY ERIC'S PARENTS GAVE HIM AN ACOUSTIC GUITAR. IT WAS CHEAP AND DIFFICULT TO PLAY SO IT TOOK HIM A WHILE TO GET STARTED. (1958)   BUT ...

WHEN HE WAS 15 ERIC GOT SERIOUS ABOUT PLAYING AFTER HEARING AMERICAN BLUES RECORDS BY ROBERT JOHNSON, B.B. KING, FREDDIE KING, ALBERT KING, BUDDY GUY, MUDDY WATERS, AND HOWLIN' WOLF. THEY WERE HIS HEROES WHEN HE WAS YOUNG.

ERIC PRACTICED FOR HOURS AND HOURS PLAYING ALONG TO HIS BLUES RECORDS. HE RECORDED HIMSELF PLAYING LICKS OVER AND OVER WITH A REEL-TO-REEL TAPE RECORDER. HE WOULD LISTEN BACK AND PRACTICE UNTIL HE FELT HE'D GOT IT RIGHT.

WHEN HE WAS 16 ERIC WENT TO ART COLLEGE BUT WAS DISMISSED AT THE END OF THE YEAR BECAUSE HE PLAYED HIS GUITAR MORE THAN HE WENT TO SCHOOL.

ERIC BEGAN BUSKING (PLAYING IN THE STREET FOR CHANGE) AROUND THE WEST END OF LONDON. HE PLAYED ALL THE BLUES SONGS THAT HE KNEW.

WHEN HE WAS 17, ERIC STARTED PERFORMING IN THE PUBS AROUND HIS HOMETOWN. HIS GUITAR PLAYING WAS SO ADVANCED BY THAT TIME THAT HE STARTED GETTING NOTICED. (1962)

IN 1963 ERIC JOINED HIS FIRST BAND, "THE ROOSTERS." WHEN THAT ENDED HE PLAYED WITH "CASEY JONES & THE ENGINEERS." FROM THERE HE WAS ASKED TO JOIN "THE YARDBIRDS."

ERIC WAS 18 WHEN HE JOINED THE UP-AND-COMING YARDBIRDS. EVERYONE CONSIDERED ERIC TO BE THE BEST GUITARIST ON THE BRITISH BLUES MUSIC SCENE.

WHEN HE WAS 19, ERIC TOURED AND RECORDED TWO ALBUMS WITH THE YARDBIRDS.

ERIC WAS 20 WHEN THE YARDBIRDS HAD THEIR FIRST MAJOR HIT, "FOR YOUR LOVE." (1965) HE DECIDED TO LEAVE THE BAND BECAUSE AT THAT TIME HE ONLY WANTED TO PLAY THE BLUES.

MAKE YOUR GUITAR SCREAM AND CRY!!!

Add **feeling** and **emotion** to your playing by **bending strings** and sustaining notes with **vibrato** – give some "life" to that note by bending it and shaking it!

BENDING

Proper Bending Technique >

Most of the time you will bend with your 3rd or 4th finger. Reinforce the 3rd finger with your 2nd and 1st fingers. Reinforce the 4th finger (pinkie) with your 3rd and 2nd fingers. **Really get under it and push it up!**

You can bend a half-step up, a whole-step up, a step-and-a-half up... Make sure your intonation (pitch) is correct. To develop intonation – **play** the note that you are intending to bend up to, **keep it** fresh in your mind, then **bend** the string up to the **proper pitch.** Push up on the high strings. Pull down on the low.

Turn up the volume on your amp. Face your guitar at the amp and bend up to the note you want to play. (Get it up there and hold it up there!) Find the "sweet spot" where you can bend up to the note, hold it, and make it feedback and sustain forever!!!

SHAKE IT! VIBRATO

Shake the string and make it sing!

Technically vibrato is a series of small bends. What you're doing is pushing and pulling up and down on the string very rapidly to change the pitch ever so slightly.

Typically you will hold the note with your 1st or 3rd finger and then "shake" your wrist sideways to move the string.

You can create different types of vibrato by shaking your hand, your wrist, or even your whole arm (like Stevie Ray Vaughan).

The speed and width of your vibrato is what determines your unique style.

How long can you hold a note without vibrato? How much longer can you hold it with vibrato?

Joe Perry

ANTHONY JOSEPH PEREIRA WAS BORN ON SEPTEMBER 10, 1950 IN LAWRENCE, MA.

WHEN JOE WAS 6 YEARS OLD, HE LISTENED TO HIS NEIGHBOR'S EARLY ROCK N' ROLL RECORDS. (1956) HE HEARD SONGS BY ELVIS PRESLEY, LITTLE RICHARD, AND CHUCK BERRY.

JOE GOT SERIOUS ABOUT PLAYING THE GUITAR WHEN HE WAS 14 YEARS OLD AFTER SEEING THE BEATLES ON THE ED SULLIVAN SHOW. (1964)

JOE WAS THEN INSPIRED BY BRITISH BANDS LIKE THE ROLLING STONES, THE YARDBIRDS, FLEETWOOD MAC, CREAM, AND LED ZEPPELIN. JIMI HENDRIX WAS ALSO A HUGE INFLUENCE ON JOE. (1967)

IN HIGH SCHOOL JOE PLAYED IN BANDS CALLED "FLASH," "JUST US," AND "PLASTIC GLASS." (1968) WHEN HE WAS 18 HE FORMED A BAND WITH TOM HAMILTON ON BASS CALLED "THE JAM BAND."

THE BAD BOY FROM BOSTON

JOE WAS 19 YEARS OLD WHEN HE MET STEVEN TYLER IN SUNAPEE, NEW HAMPSHIRE AT A PLACE CALLED "THE BARN" WHERE EACH OF THEIR BANDS WERE PLAYING. (1969)

AFTER GUITARIST BRAD WHITFORD AND DRUMMER JOEY KRAMER JOINED THE BAND, JOE, STEVEN, AND TOM MOVED TO BOSTON AND THEY BECAME AEROSMITH. (1970)

AEROSMITH PLAYED 100'S OF GIGS AT CLUBS AND COLLEGES ALL AROUND NEW ENGLAND AND THE NEW YORK AREA FOR THE NEXT TWO YEARS. JOE WAS 22 WHEN AEROSMITH WAS DISCOVERED PLAYING AT 'MAX'S KANSAS CITY' IN NEW YORK CITY. (1972)

JOE WAS 23 YEARS OLD WHEN AEROSMITH RECORDED THEIR FIRST ALBUM IN 1973.

ROCK RIFFS

THESE ARE ALL GREAT RIFFS. ONE THING THAT MAKES MANY OF THESE RIFFS GREAT IS THAT THEY ARE EASY TO PLAY. THE RIFF IS OFTEN THE "HOOK" – THE PART OF THE SONG YOU REMEMBER.

15 RIFFS FROM THE 60'S
- PURPLE HAZE – JIMI HENDRIX
- FOXY LADY – JIMI HENDRIX
- FIRE – JIMI HENDRIX
- VOODOO CHILD – JIMI HENDRIX
- SATISFACTION – THE ROLLING STONES
- JUMPIN' JACK FLASH – ROLLING STONES
- SUNSHINE OF YOUR LOVE – CREAM
- TRAIN KEPT A ROLLIN' – THE YARDBIRDS
- DAY TRIPPER – THE BEATLES
- YOU REALLY GOT ME – THE KINKS
- BREAK ON THROUGH – THE DOORS
- I'M A MAN – SPENCER DAVIS GROUP
- BORN TO BE WILD – STEPPENWOLF
- IN-A-GADDA-DA-VIDA – IRON BUTTERFLY
- PINBALL WIZARD – THE WHO
- OH, PRETTY WOMAN – ROY ORBISON

20 LED ZEPPELIN RIFFS
- WHOLE LOTTA LOVE
- BLACK DOG
- BRING IT ON HOME
- DAZED AND CONFUSED
- THE OCEAN
- HEARTBREAKER
- LIVIN' LOVIN' MAID
- HOW MANY MORE TIMES
- IMMIGRANT SONG
- KASHMIR
- MISTY MOUNTAIN HOP
- THE ROVER
- WHEN THE LEVEE BREAKS
- NO QUARTER
- ROCK AND ROLL
- THE LEMON SONG
- MOBY DICK
- THE WANTON SONG
- TRAMPLED UNDER FOOT
- FOUR STICKS

5 AEROSMITH RIFFS
- WALK THIS WAY
- RATS IN THE CELLAR
- SAME OLD STORY
- SWEET EMOTION
- LAST CHILD

5 AC/DC RIFFS
- BACK IN BLACK
- HIGHWAY TO HELL
- WHOLE LOTTA ROSIE
- HELLS BELLS
- THUNDERSTRUCK

5 VAN HALEN RIFFS
- AIN'T TALKIN' 'BOUT LOVE
- MEAN STREET
- UNCHAINED
- HOT FOR TEACHER
- PANAMA

25 RIFFS FROM THE 70'S
- SMOKE ON THE WATER – DEEP PURPLE
- ROCK CANDY – MONTROSE
- BARRACUDA – HEART
- MONEY – PINK FLOYD
- SLOW RIDE – FOGHAT
- CARRY ON WAYWARD SON – KANSAS
- ROADHOUSE BLUES – THE DOORS
- SCHOOL'S OUT – ALICE COOPER
- SATURDAY NITE SPECIAL – LYNYRD SKYNYRD
- ROCK STEADY – BAD COMPANY
- GODZILLA – BLUE OYSTER CULT
- FRANKENSTEIN – EDGAR WINTER GROUP
- STONE COLD CRAZY – QUEEN
- JAILBREAK – THIN LIZZY
- LAYLA – DEREK AND THE DOMINOS
- LIFE IN THE FAST LANE – THE EAGLES
- MISSISSIPPI QUEEN – MOUNTAIN
- AQUALUNG – JETHRO TULL
- ROUNDABOUT – YES
- BRIDGE OF SIGHS – ROBIN TROWER
- ROCKY MOUNTAIN WAY – JOE WALSH
- CAT SCRATCH FEVER – TED NUGENT
- JEEPSTER – T. REX
- ROCK BOTTOM – UFO
- JUST GOT PAID – ZZ TOP

LEARN TO PLAY 'EM ALL!

15 MODERN ROCK RIFFS
- SEVEN NATION ARMY – THE WHITE STRIPES
- SMELLS LIKE TEEN SPIRIT – NIRVANA
- MAN IN THE BOX – ALICE IN CHAINS
- SLITHER – VELVET REVOLVER
- EVEN FLOW – PEARL JAM
- OUTSHINED – SOUNDGARDEN
- NO ONE KNOWS – QUEENS OF THE STONE AGE
- BEEN CAUGHT STEALING – JANE'S ADDICTION
- UNDER THE BRIDGE – RED HOT CHILI PEPPERS
- BULLS ON PARADE – RAGE AGAINST THE MACHINE
- TOXICITY – SYSTEM OF A DOWN
- BIG BANG BABY – STONE TEMPLE PILOTS
- PARANOID ANDROID – RADIOHEAD
- PLUG IN BABY – MUSE
- MY OWN SUMMER – DEFTONES

GO TO WWW.ULTIMATE-GUITAR.COM TO GET THE TABS.
GO TO YOUTUBE.COM TO SEE HOW TO PLAY THE RIFFS.

Stevie Ray Vaughan

STEPHEN RAY VAUGHAN WAS BORN ON OCTOBER 3, 1954 IN DALLAS, TEXAS.

WHEN STEVIE TURNED 7 YEARS OLD HIS FATHER BOUGHT HIM A TOY ACOUSTIC GUITAR FOR HIS BIRTHDAY. STEVIE'S OLDER BROTHER, JIMMIE, SHOWED STEVIE HOW TO PLAY A FEW BASIC CHORDS. (1961)

STEVIE'S FIRST ELECTRIC GUITAR – A GIFT FROM JIMMIE – WAS A GIBSON 125T. (1963)

WHEN STEVIE WAS IN HIGH SCHOOL HE PRACTICED GUITAR AT LEAST 5 HOURS A DAY AND PLAYED IN A BUNCH OF BANDS.

STEVIE'S BIGGEST INFLUENCES WERE HIS OLDER BROTHER JIMMIE, JIMI HENDRIX, AND BLUESMAN ALBERT KING. (1967)

STEVIE BOUGHT HIS FIRST FENDER STRATOCASTER WHEN HE WAS 16 YEARS OLD. (1970)

THE TEXAS TORNADO

WHEN STEVIE WAS 17 HE MOVED TO AUSTIN, TEXAS.

WHEN STEVIE WAS 18 HE JOINED "THE NIGHTCRAWLERS." THEY RECORDED AN ALBUM IN LOS ANGELES AND TOURED THE U.S. OPENING FOR HUMBLE PIE AND THE J. GEILS BAND. (1972)

STEVIE WAS 19 WHEN HE GOT THE '63 STRATOCASTER HE USED FOR THE REST OF HIS CAREER.

WHILE IN HIS EARLY 20'S STEVIE PLAYED OVER 1,000 GIGS IN AND AROUND AUSTIN, TX.

STEVIE WAS 25 YEARS OLD WHEN HE FORMED THE BAND "DOUBLE TROUBLE" WITH FORMER BANDMATES TOMMY SHANNON ON BASS AND CHRIS LAYTON ON DRUMS. (1979)

STEVIE'S PERFORMANCE AT THE 1982 MONTREUX JAZZ FESTIVAL IMPRESSED DAVID BOWIE SO MUCH HE HIRED STEVIE TO PLAY ON HIS "LET'S DANCE" RECORD.

STEVIE WAS 29 WHEN HE RECORDED HIS FIRST ALBUM, "TEXAS FLOOD" IN 1983.

THE BLUES

Most rock n' roll and classic rock is based on the blues. Because it is the basis for so much music, learning the blues is an important step in learning to play guitar.

The blues has its origins in the musical traditions of the West African people brought to America as slaves. The work songs, field hollers, and spirituals of the African-American communities in the southern United States eventually evolved into the blues.

In the **1940's** many African-Americans moved to the cities in the north where there were jobs in factories. The blues musicians who moved north started using electric guitars and amplifiers to be heard in the loud, crowded nightclubs where they played.

In the **1950's** rock n' roll evolved from the blues. As Muddy Waters said, "The blues had a baby, and they named the baby rock n' roll."

5 CLASSIC BLUES RIFFS
I'm A Man – Muddy Waters
You Shook Me – Muddy Waters
Hoochie Coochie Man – Muddy Waters
Boom Boom – John Lee Hooker
Born Under A Bad Sign – Albert King

In the **1960's** a small group of young English musicians got their start playing the blues. The Rolling Stones, The Yardbirds, Led Zeppelin, and many others were deeply influenced by the blues. They recorded covers of blues songs and exposed young rock audiences to the blues.

12 BAR BLUES – The most common blues chord progression is the 12 bar blues. Learn the 12 bar blues and when you jam with other musicians one guitarist can play the chords and the other guitarist can play lead. Then you can switch.

Use the sections on the pentatonic scales to learn how to play lead over the 12 bar blues.

12 BAR BLUES – KEY OF A

	A5	A5	A5	A5
D5	D5	A5	A5
E5	D5	A5	E5	

"YOU JUST NEED TO PRACTICE MORE..."

A5
```
E|----------------
B|----------------
G|----------------
D|2 2 4 4 2 2 4 4
A|0 0 0 0 0 0 0 0
E|----------------
```

D5
```
E|----------------
B|----------------
G|2 2 4 4 2 2 4 4
D|0 0 0 0 0 0 0 0
A|----------------
E|----------------
```

E5
```
E|----------------
B|----------------
G|----------------
D|----------------
A|2 2 4 4 2 2 4 4
E|0 0 0 0 0 0 0 0
```

Tony Iommi

FRANCIS ANTHONY IOMMI WAS BORN ON FERUARY 19, 1948 IN BIRMINGHAM, ENGLAND.

TONY STARTED PLAYING THE GUITAR WHEN HE WAS 12 YEARS OLD AFTER BEING INSPIRED BY HANK MARVIN, THE GUITAR PLAYER FROM THE BAND "THE SHADOWS." (1960)

TONY PLAYED IN SEVERAL BLUES/ROCK BANDS WHEN HE WAS A TEENAGER. WHEN HE WAS 17 HIS BAND WAS OFFERED A REGULAR GIG IN GERMANY. (1965)

TONY WORKED IN A SHEET METAL FACTORY AND ON HIS LAST DAY OF WORK BEFORE LEAVING FOR GERMANY, HE CUT OFF THE TIPS OF HIS MIDDLE AND RING FINGERS ON HIS RIGHT HAND IN AN ACCIDENT. HE PLAYS GUITAR LEFT-HANDED SO THIS WAS VERY BAD.

TONY THOUGHT ABOUT GIVING UP PLAYING GUITAR, BUT RECONSIDERED AFTER HEARING GYPSY JAZZ GUITARIST DJANGO REINHARDT, WHO LOST THE USE OF TWO OF HIS FINGERS IN A CAMPFIRE ACCIDENT.

TO MAKE PLAYING EASIER, TONY STRUNG HIS GUITARS WITH EXTRA-LIGHT STRINGS AND PUT PLASTIC COVERS OVER THE TWO DAMAGED FINGERS. (1966)

IN 1967, WHEN TONY WAS 19, HE FORMED A BAND CALLED "EARTH" WITH THREE OLD FRIENDS FROM SCHOOL - TERRY "GEEZER" BUTLER ON BASS, BILL WARD ON DRUMS, AND JOHN "OZZY" OSBOURNE ON VOCALS.

WHEN TONY WAS 20 YEARS OLD HE JOINED THE BAND "JETHRO TULL." HE PLAYED WITH THEM ON THE ROLLING STONES' ROCK N' ROLL CIRCUS TV SPECIAL, BUT HE SOON LEFT TO REJOIN EARTH.

THE GODFATHER OF METAL

AFTER TONY CAME BACK, EARTH CHANGED THEIR NAME TO "BLACK SABBATH." (1969)

AT FIRST TONY PLAYED A FENDER STRATOCASTER. WHEN ONE OF THE PICKUPS ON THE STRAT STOPPED WORKING TONY SWITCHED TO USING HIS BACK-UP GUITAR, A GIBSON SG.

TONY WAS 21 YEARS OLD WHEN BLACK SABBATH RECORDED THEIR FIRST ALBUM IN 1970.

METAL

Black Sabbath is the first true metal band. Their tone, technique, riffs (using tritones, chromatic progressions, and pedal tones), volume, and dark lyrics and imagery have defined metal since their first album, "Black Sabbath." (1970)

Judas Priest introduced harmonized dual lead guitars, a tight metallic tone, and chord progressions not based on the blues. Judas Priest also increased the tempo and made it faster. Motörhead mixed in punk rock attitude and aggression and increased the tempo. Iron Maiden and the other New Wave of British Heavy Metal (NWOBHM) bands emphasized speed and precision. The NWOBHM inspired bands like Metallica, who increased the tempo to create thrash and speed metal, which influenced styles like death metal, black metal, nü-metal, metal core, etc...

METAL TECHNIQUE

Your picking hand technique is crucial when playing metal....

PALM MUTING – Lightly rest the side of your picking hand on the strings close to the bridge to mute the strings and create a percussive "chugging" sound.

DOWN STROKES VS. ALTERNATING UP AND DOWN – Using downstrokes creates a very aggressive feel to the rhythm. James Hetfield uses downstrokes almost exclusively.

METAL TONE

To get a crunchy metal tone, turn up the "gain" knob on your amp (or use a distortion pedal), turn down the "mids" knob on the amp, use some delay, and turn the volume on your guitar all the way up.

METAL GUITAR SOLOS

Metal guitar players often play solos based on the modes. (See the next section.) The Aeolian and Phrygian modes are the most commonly used in metal because they sound dark and ominous. Tony Iommi from Black Sabbath uses the Dorian mode a lot. Randy Rhoads and Yngwie Malmsteen use the classical sounding harmonic minor scale. These scales make "shredding" possible because you play three-notes-per-string.

10 BLACK SABBATH RIFFS
Sabbath Bloody Sabbath
Symptom of the Universe
Children of the Grave
Black Sabbath
Hole in the Sky
Into the Void
Iron Man
Paranoid
War Pigs
N.I.B.

5 METALLICA RIFFS
Enter Sandman
Master of Puppets
Seek and Destroy
For Whom the Bell Tolls
Sad But True

15 METAL RIFFS
Crazy Train – Ozzy Osbourne
Welcome to the Jungle – Guns N' Roses
Breaking the Law – Judas Priest
Ace of Spades – Motörhead
Cowboys from Hell – Pantera
Cemetery Gates – Pantera
Walk – Pantera
Holy Diver – Dio
Hangar 18 – Megadeth
Tornado of Souls – Megadeth
Raining Blood – Slayer
Thrown to the Wolves – Death Angel
The Number of the Beast – Iron Maiden
The Trooper – Iron Maiden
Madhouse – Anthrax

ATTACK YOUR STRINGS!

THE MODES

THE SEVEN MODES CORRESPOND TO THE SEVEN NOTES OF THE MAJOR SCALE. THE NOTE YOU BEGIN WITH DETERMINES THE MODE YOU ARE IN. FOR INSTANCE, IF YOU START PLAYING FROM THE 3RD NOTE OF THE MAJOR SCALE YOU WILL BE IN THE PHRYGIAN MODE. IF YOU START PLAYING FROM THE 6TH NOTE OF THE MAJOR SCALE YOU WILL BE IN THE AEOLIAN MODE.

THIS IS BECAUSE THE **INTERVALS** (THE SPACES) BETWEEN THE NOTES CHANGES DEPENDING ON THE NOTE YOU BEGIN WITH. THE DIFFERENT INTERVAL PATTERNS ARE WHAT DEFINES THE MODES AND GIVES THE INDIVIDUAL MODES THEIR UNIQUE SOUND AND CHARACTER.

THE INTERVAL PATTERNS ALSO DETERMINE THE FINGERING PATTERNS USED TO PLAY THE MODES. THERE ARE **SEVEN FINGERING PATTERNS** WHICH ARE **COMMON TO ALL 7 MODES** – THE ONLY DIFFERENCE IS WHICH NOTE WITHIN THE SCALE YOU USE AS THE ROOT.

THE 7 FINGERING PATTERNS ALL HAVE **3 NOTES PER STRING** – PLAY THESE PATTERNS TO "SHRED."

HERE IS HOW THE **MAJOR SCALE** LOOKS IN THE **KEY OF C**... (ROOT NOTE ON THE 6TH STRING, 8TH FRET) NOTICE HOW THE PATTERNS CONNECT TO EACH OTHER AND HOW THEY REPEAT EVERY 12 FRETS...

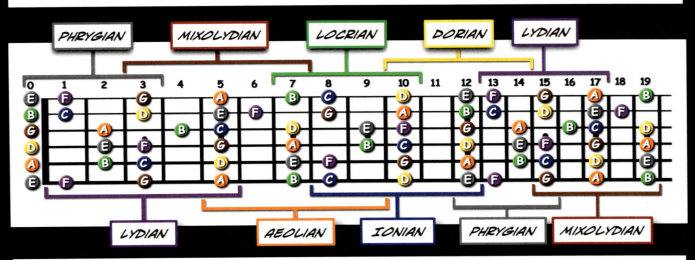

EACH MODE HAS IT'S OWN "MOOD." (MODE = MOOD)
TO ESTABLISH THE SOUND ~ MOOD ~ OF A MODE ...
A) EMPHASIZE **THE ROOT** OF THE SCALE ~ MAKE THIS NOTE FEEL LIKE HOME.
B) EMPHASIZE **THE 3RD** ~ THIS NOTE GIVES THE MODE IT'S MAJOR OR MINOR QUALITY.
C) EMPHASIZE **THE CHARACTERISTIC NOTE** ~ THIS NOTE GIVES THE MODE IT'S UNIQUE SOUND.

THE MODES IN ORDER OF "BRIGHTEST" TO "DARKEST":
LYDIAN, IONIAN, MIXOLYDIAN, DORIAN, AEOLIAN, PHRYGIAN, LOCRIAN

THE MODES IN ORDER OF POPULARITY IN MODERN MUSIC:
IONIAN, AEOLIAN, MIXOLYDIAN, DORIAN, PHRYGIAN, LYDIAN, LOCRIAN

IONIAN

THE MAJOR SCALE
"BRIGHT" "VIBRANT" "HAPPY"

THE MAJOR SCALE IS THE FOUNDATION OF ALL WESTERN MUSIC. THE OTHER SCALES AND MODES ARE ALL BASED ON THE MAJOR SCALE.

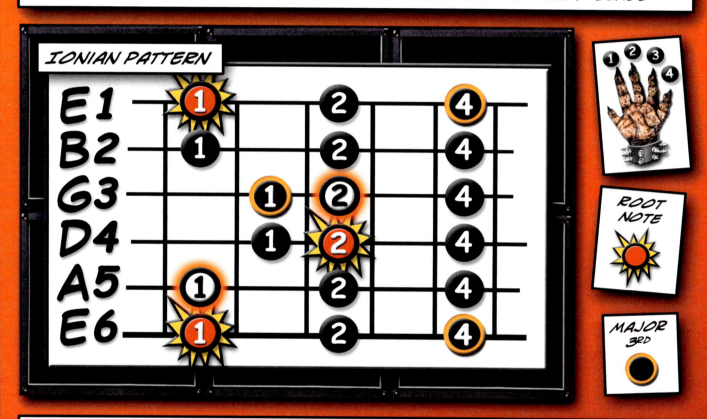

THE CHARACTERISTIC NOTE OF THE IONIAN MODE IS THE 4TH.
HOLDING THE 4TH DOES NOT SOUND HARMONIOUS. THE 4TH WORKS BEST AS A PASSING TONE. USE HAMMER-ONS AND PULL-OFFS TO TOUCH ON THE 4TH BEFORE QUICKLY RESOLVING BACK TO THE 3RD.

THE IONIAN MODE IS THE FIRST OF THE SEVEN MUSICAL MODES. IT IS THE SCALE THAT APPEARS WHEN THE MAJOR SCALE IS PLAYED STARTING FROM THE 1ST NOTE (FIRST SCALE-DEGREE): C

INTERVAL FORMULA:

ROOT 2 3 4 5 6 7 OCTAVE
W   W H W W W H

DORIAN

"SOULFUL" "SMOOTH"

● THE DORIAN MODE IS A MINOR SCALE.

THE DORIAN MODE IS A GOOD ALTERNATIVE TO THE COMMON MINOR SCALE (THE AEOLIAN MODE). IT IS NOT AS "DARK" AS THE OTHER MINOR MODES (THE AEOLIAN AND PHRYGIAN MODES).

THE DORIANS, IONIANS, AND AEOLIANS WERE THE MAJOR TRIBES IN GREECE 3000 YEARS AGO.

TO THE ANCIENT GREEKS THE DORIAN MODE CORRESPONDED TO THE ELEMENT OF WATER.

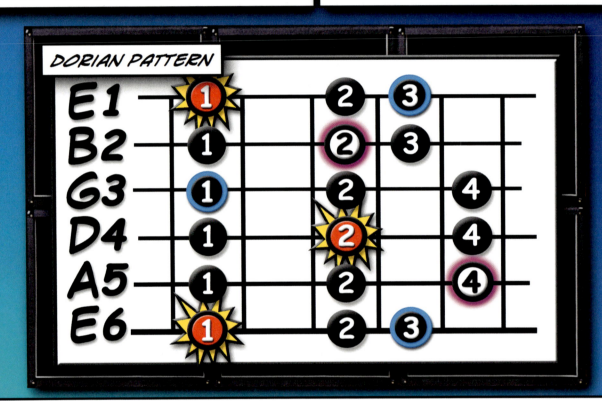

DORIAN PATTERN

THE CHARACTERISTIC NOTE OF THE DORIAN MODE IS THE 6TH.

○ THE 6TH HAS A DUAL PERSONALITY – IT CAN BE USED AS A PASSING TONE OR HELD TO CREATE TENSION. THE TENSION OF THE 6TH IS NOT SO GREAT THAT YOU CAN'T HOLD IT (UNLIKE THE 4TH IN THE IONIAN MODE). IT ALSO WORKS GOOD AS A LANDING NOTE – YOU CAN PLAY THE 6TH WHEN CHANGING BACK TO A MINOR CHORD.

THE DORIAN MODE IS THE SECOND OF THE SEVEN MUSICAL MODES. IT IS THE SCALE THAT APPEARS WHEN THE MAJOR SCALE IS PLAYED STARTING FROM THE 2ND NOTE (SECOND SCALE-DEGREE): D

INTERVAL FORMULA:

ROOT 2 b3 4 5 6 b7 OCTAVE

W H W W W H W

PHRYGIAN

"GLOOMY" "SPANISH"

TO THE ANCIENT GREEKS THE PHRYGIAN MODE CORRESPONDED TO THE ELEMENT OF *FIRE*. THEY BELIEVED IT PROMOTED BOLDNESS AND PASSION.

THE PHRYGIAN MODE IS COMMON IN FLAMENCO MUSIC AND IS THEREFORE REFERRED TO AS THE "SPANISH" MODE. IT IS NOW USED FOR SHREDDING METAL SOLOS.

- THE PHRYGIAN MODE IS A MINOR SCALE.

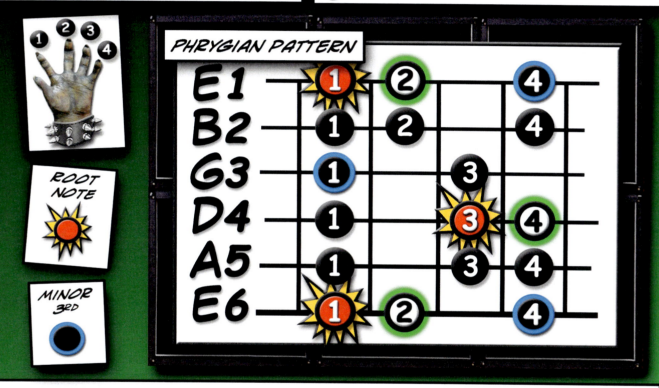

THE CHARACTERISTIC NOTE OF THE PHRYGIAN MODE IS THE FLATTED 2ND. THE DISTANCE BETWEEN THE FLAT 2ND AND THE ROOT (1ST) IS ONLY A HALF-STEP APART. THIS RELATIONSHIP CREATES THE UNIQUE SOUND OF THE PHRYGIAN MODE. THE FLAT 2ND OFTEN WORKS BEST AS A PASSING TONE. USE HAMMER-ONS AND PULL-OFFS TO TOUCH ON THE FLAT 2ND BEFORE QUICKLY RESOLVING BACK TO THE ROOT NOTE (1ST).

WHEN PLAYING IN THE PHRYGIAN MODE MANY MUSICIANS DO NOT PLAY THE FLATTED 3RD (THE MINOR 3RD) BECAUSE LEAVING IT OUT PUTS MORE EMPHASIS ON THE FLATTED 2ND AND THE UNIQUE MOOD IT CREATES. USE THE FLATTED 6TH AS A PASSING TONE ALSO.

THE PHRYGIAN MODE IS THE THIRD OF THE SEVEN MUSICAL MODES. IT IS THE SCALE THAT APPEARS WHEN THE MAJOR SCALE IS PLAYED STARTING FROM THE 3RD NOTE (THIRD SCALE-DEGREE): E

INTERVAL FORMULA:

ROOT b2 b3 4 5 b6 b7 OCTAVE
     H W W W H W W

LYDIAN

"AIRY" "ETHEREAL" "WISTFUL"

 THE LYDIAN MODE IS A MAJOR SCALE.

THE LYDIAN MODE IS THE "LIGHTEST" SOUNDING MODE.

NAMED AFTER THE KINGDOM OF LYDIA BY ANCIENT GREEK MUSICIANS.

TO THE ANCIENT GREEKS THE LYDIAN MODE CORRESPONDED TO THE ELEMENT OF **AIR**.

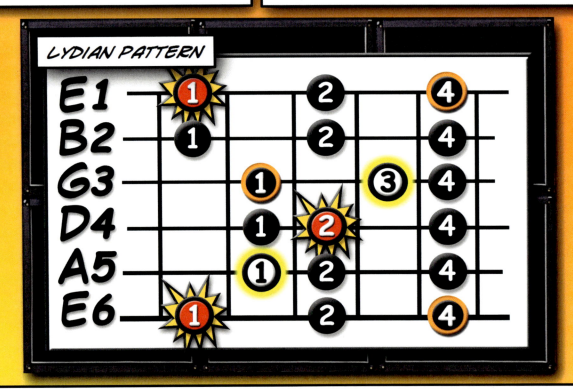

LYDIAN PATTERN

THE CHARACTERISTIC NOTE OF THE LYDIAN MODE IS THE SHARP 4TH. THE SHARP 4TH GIVES THE LYDIAN MODE A SPACEY, UNRESOLVED QUALITY. THE BEAUTY OF THE #4 IS THAT IT CAN BE HELD OVER A MAJOR CHORD WITHOUT SOUNDING HARSH. BUT DON'T OVER USE IT! RESOLVE FROM THE #4 TO A MORE STABLE TONE – THE MAJOR 3RD.

THE LYDIAN MODE IS THE FOURTH OF THE SEVEN MUSICAL MODES. IT IS THE SCALE THAT APPEARS WHEN THE MAJOR SCALE IS PLAYED STARTING FROM THE 4TH NOTE (FOURTH SCALE-DEGREE): F

INTERVAL FORMULA:

ROOT 2 3 #4 5 6 7 OCTAVE

W W W H W W H

MIXOLYDIAN

"FUNKY" OR "FOLKY"

 THE MIXOLYDIAN MODE IS A MAJOR SCALE.

THE MIXOLYDIAN MODE IS LIKE A GRITTIER VERSION OF THE MAJOR SCALE.

TO THE ANCIENT GREEKS THE MIXOLYDIAN MODE CORRESPONDED TO THE ELEMENT OF **EARTH**.

THE MIXOLYDIAN MODE HAS BEEN USED IN A LOT OF CLASSIC ROCK SONGS. LISTEN TO LYNYRD SKYNYRD'S "SWEET HOME ALABAMA" OR VAN HALEN'S "I'M THE ONE."

ROOT NOTE

MAJOR 3RD

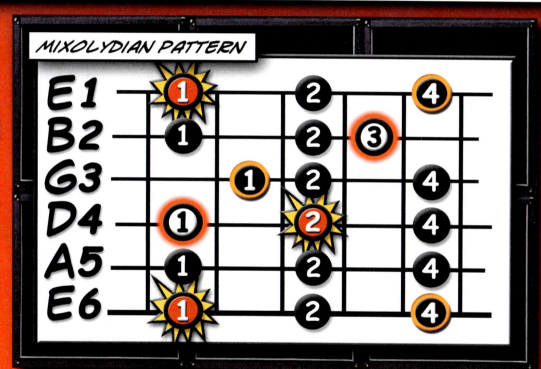
MIXOLYDIAN PATTERN

THE CHARACTERISTIC NOTE OF THE MIXOLYDIAN MODE IS THE FLATTED 7TH. BY USING THE FLATTED 7TH YOU CAN GET A VERY BLUESY, COUNTRY SOUND. THE FLATTED 7TH CAN BE HELD AT LENGTH OVER A MAJOR CHORD WITHOUT SOUNDING TOO TENSE. LISTEN TO THE DIFFERENCE BETWEEN A MAJOR CHORD (G) AND A SEVENTH CHORD (G7). THAT IS THE DIFFERENCE BETWEEN THE IONIAN MODE AND THE MIXOLYDIAN MODE.

THE MIXOLYDIAN MODE IS THE FIFTH OF THE SEVEN MUSICAL MODES. IT IS THE SCALE THAT APPEARS WHEN THE MAJOR SCALE IS PLAYED STARTING FROM THE 5TH NOTE (FIFTH SCALE-DEGREE): G

INTERVAL FORMULA:

ROOT 2 3 4 5 6 b7 OCTAVE
W W H W W H W

AEOLIAN

THE AEOLIAN MODE IS USED TO EXPRESS **SORROW AND PAIN**.

THE "SADDEST" OF ALL THE MODES.

THE NATURAL MINOR SCALE

AEOLIAN PATTERN

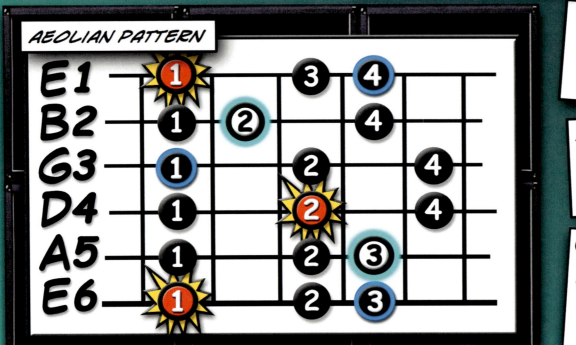

ROOT NOTE

MINOR 3RD

THE CHARACTERISTIC NOTE OF THE AEOLIAN MODE IS THE FLATTED 6TH. THE FLAT 6TH IS BEST USED AS A PASSING TONE. IF YOU HOLD THE FLAT 6TH OVER A MINOR CHORD IT CREATES AN UNHARMONIOUS SENSE OF TENSION. ALTHOUGH IT MAY BE HELD OCCASIONALLY TO CREATE AN ATMOSPHERIC, OMINOUS EFFECT, USUALLY YOU WILL USE HAMMER-ONS AND PULL-OFFS TO TOUCH BRIEFLY ON THE FLAT 6TH. MERGING THE FLAT 6TH INTO A LARGER PHRASE PUTS IT INTO CONTEXT AND REMOVES THE UNHARMONIOUS TENSION.

THE AEOLIAN MODE IS THE SIXTH OF THE SEVEN MUSICAL MODES. IT IS THE SCALE THAT APPEARS WHEN THE MAJOR SCALE IS PLAYED STARTING FROM THE 6TH NOTE (SIXTH SCALE-DEGREE): A

INTERVAL FORMULA:

ROOT 2 b3 4 5 b6 b7 OCTAVE
   W H W W H W W

Locrian

"SINISTER" "DARK"

THE LOCRIAN MODE IS CONSIDERED THE "DARKEST" OF ALL THE MODES.

THE DISSONANCE, OR MUSICAL IMBALANCE, OF THE LOCRIAN MODE CREATES A SENSE OF OVERALL TENSION.

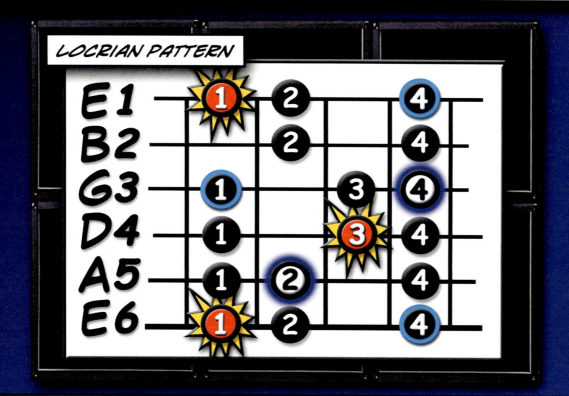

◯ THE CHARACTERISTIC NOTE OF THE LOCRIAN MODE IS THE FLATTED 5TH.

THE TONIC (1ST) CHORD THAT IS BUILT FROM THE LOCRIAN MODE IS A *DIMINISHED TRIAD* BECAUSE IT HAS A MINOR 3RD AND A DIMINISHED 5TH (FLATTED 5TH). DUE TO THE FLATTED 5TH IT LACKS TONAL CENTER AND IS CONSIDERED DISSONANT AND UNSTABLE. THEREFORE, YOU WILL NOT FIND SONGS WRITTEN IN THE LOCRIAN MODE VERY OFTEN.

THE LOCRIAN MODE IS THE SEVENTH OF THE SEVEN MUSICAL MODES. IT IS THE SCALE THAT APPEARS WHEN THE MAJOR SCALE IS PLAYED STARTING FROM THE 7TH NOTE (SEVENTH SCALE-DEGREE): B

INTERVAL FORMULA:
ROOT b2 b3 4 b5 b6 b7 OCTAVE
  H   W W H W W W

THE SEVEN MODES COMPLETE

THE 4TH
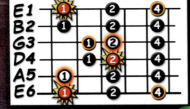
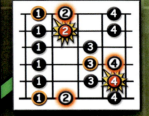

THE 6TH

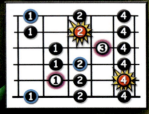

THE FLATTED 2ND
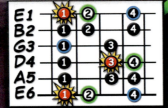
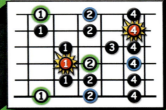
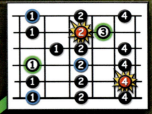

THE SHARP 4TH
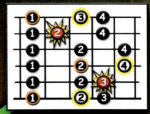

MIXOLYDIAN
THE FLATTED 7TH

AEOLIAN
THE FLATTED 6TH

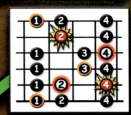

LOCRIAN
THE FLATTED 5TH

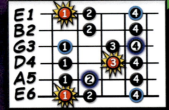

THIS MAY APPEAR COMPLICATED BUT IT'S NOT. THESE SEVEN SCALES SHARE THE SAME SEVEN INTERLOCKING PATTERNS. THE DIFFERENCE IS WHERE THE ROOT NOTES FALL.

Randy Rhoads

RANDALL WILLIAM RHOADS WAS BORN ON DECEMBER 6, 1956 IN SANTA MONICA, CA.

WHEN RANDY WAS 6 YEARS OLD HE STARTED TAKING GUITAR LESSONS AT THE MUSIC SCHOOL HIS MOTHER, DELORES, OWNED AND RAN IN NORTH HOLLYWOOD.

RANDY'S FIRST GUITAR WAS A GIBSON ACOUSTIC THAT BELONGED TO HIS GRANDFATHER. (1962)

RANDY BECAME INTERESTED IN PLAYING ROCK GUITAR WHEN HE WAS 12 YEARS OLD. (1969) HIS MOTHER GAVE HIM AN OLD SEMI-ACOUSTIC GUITAR THAT WAS "ALMOST AS BIG AS HE WAS."

WHEN RANDY WAS 13 YEARS OLD HE STOPPED TAKING GUITAR LESSONS BECAUSE HE HAD ALREADY LEARNED EVERYTHING HIS TEACHERS KNEW.

RANDY FORMED HIS FIRST BAND, "VIOLET FOX," WHEN HE WAS 14. (1971) RANDY PLAYED GUITAR AND HIS OLDER BROTHER, KELLE, PLAYED THE DRUMS.

MICK RONSON FROM DAVID BOWIE'S BAND, "THE SPIDERS FROM MARS," WAS A BIG INFLUENCE ON RANDY'S MUSIC AND LOOK.

IN HIGH SCHOOL RANDY GAVE GUITAR LESSONS AT HIS MOTHER'S MUSIC SCHOOL AND STARTED A BAND WITH HIS FRIEND KELLY GARNI ON BASS.

WHEN RANDY WAS 16 HE AND KELLY FORMED THE BAND "QUIET RIOT." (1973) QUIET RIOT PLAYED BACKYARD PARTIES AND THE CLUBS ON THE SUNSET STRIP IN HOLLYWOOD. THEY RECORDED TWO ALBUMS THAT WERE ONLY RELEASED IN JAPAN.

WHEN RANDY WAS 22, HE JOINED OZZY OSBOURNE'S BAND. (1979) HE RECORDED "THE BLIZZARD OF OZ" ALBUM AND WENT ON TOUR WITH OZZY WHEN HE WAS 23.

Harmonic Minor

THE HARMONIC MINOR SCALE IS USED TO GET A "CLASSICAL" SOUND.

THE HARMONIC MINOR IS USED BY GUITARISTS LIKE RANDY RHOADS, YNGWIE MALMSTEEN, KIRK HAMMETT, RITCHIE BLACKMORE, AND ULI JON ROTH FOR A NEO-CLASSICAL SOUND. NEO-CLASSICAL COMBINES CLASSICAL MUSIC WITH THE VOLUME AND TECHNIQUE OF ROCK AND METAL. MOZART AND BACH USED THE HARMONIC MINOR SCALE IN THEIR COMPOSITIONS ALL THE TIME.

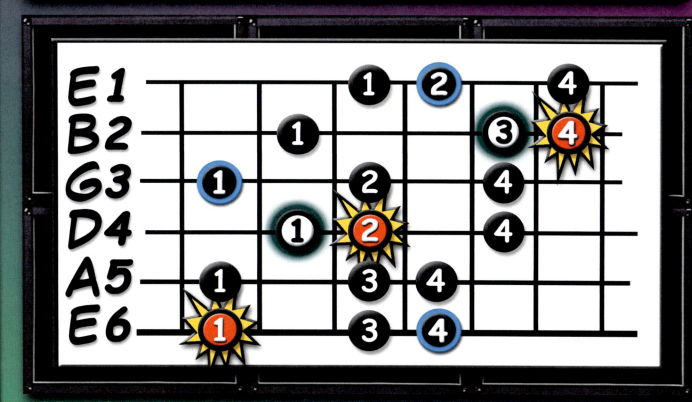

THE CHARACTERISTIC NOTE OF THE HARMONIC MINOR IS THE MAJOR 7TH. THE HARMONIC MINOR SCALE IS VERY SIMILAR TO THE AEOLIAN MODE, THE ONLY DIFFERENCE IS THAT THE HARMONIC MINOR HAS A MAJOR 7TH AND THE AEOLIAN MODE HAS A FLATTED (MINOR) 7TH. THE UNIQUE SOUND OF THE HARMONIC MINOR COMES FROM THE COMBINATION OF THE MINOR 3RD WITH THE MAJOR 7TH.

 MINOR 3RD

INTERVAL FORMULA:

ROOT 2 b3 4 5 b6 7 OCTAVE
  W H W W H W+H H

 CHECK OUT HOW SLASH USES THE HARMONIC MINOR IN THE GUITAR SOLO FOR "SWEET CHILD O' MINE."

KIRK HAMMETT

KIRK LEE HAMMETT WAS BORN ON NOVEMBER 18, 1962 IN SAN FRANCISCO, CA.

KIRK'S FIRST EXPOSURE TO ROCK MUSIC WAS THROUGH HIS OLDER BROTHER RICK'S RECORD COLLECTION WHICH INCLUDED ALBUMS BY LED ZEPPELIN, THIN LIZZY, BLACK SABBATH, UFO, DEEP PURPLE, THE ROLLING STONES, AND JIMI HENDRIX.

KIRK WOULD PLAY RICK'S GUITAR ON THE SLY WHEN RICK WASN'T HOME. WHEN KIRK WAS 15 HE GOT HIS FIRST GUITAR — A CHEAP ELECTRIC THAT CAME WITH A "SHOE BOX WITH A SPEAKER" FOR AN AMP.

IN 1978, WHEN KIRK WAS 16 YEARS OLD, HE BOUGHT A FENDER STRATOCASTER THAT HE CUSTOMIZED TO TRY TO GET THE TONE HE WANTED. HE THEN TRADED HIS STRAT FOR A USED GIBSON FLYING V.

KIRK TOOK A JOB AT A BURGER KING JUST LONG ENOUGH TO EARN THE MONEY HE NEEDED TO BUY A USED MARSHALL AMPLIFIER. (1979)

KIRK'S EARLY INFLUENCES WERE ULI JON ROTH FROM THE SCORPIONS, MICHAEL SCHENKER FROM UFO, AND ESPECIALLY JIMI HENDRIX. LATER ON KIRK WAS INFLUENCED BY BLUES PLAYERS LIKE STEVIE RAY VAUGHAN.

IN 1980, WHEN KIRK WAS 17, HE FORMED THE BAND "EXODUS" AND ESTABLISHED THE SAN FRANCISCO BAY AREA THRASH METAL SCENE WITH BANDS LIKE METALLICA, DEATH ANGEL, TESTAMENT, FORBIDDEN, POSSESSED, & VIO-LENCE SOON TO FOLLOW.

WHEN KIRK WAS 19 HE STARTED TAKING GUITAR LESSONS FROM JOE SATRIANI IN BERKELEY, CA. JOE TAUGHT KIRK ALL ABOUT THE MODES, HOW TO BUILD SCALES, "CHORD CHEMISTRY," AND MUSIC THEORY. KIRK TOOK LESSONS FROM JOE FOR 2 YEARS.

IN APRIL 1983 KIRK RECEIVED A PHONE CALL FROM THE GUYS IN METALLICA — THEY WANTED HIM TO AUDITION FOR THEIR BAND ... UHHHH... HE PASSED THE AUDITION.

KIRK WAS 20 WHEN METALLICA RECORDED THEIR FIRST ALBUM "KILL 'EM ALL" IN 1983.

METAL LICKS

GO TO WWW.THEROCKMONSTERS.COM FOR VIDEO EXAMPLES.

AEOLIAN LICKS – KEY OF A

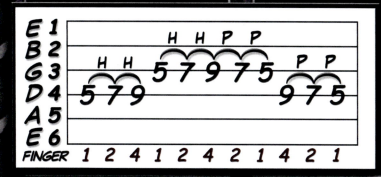
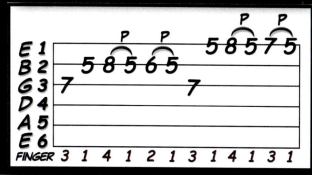

PHRYGIAN LICKS – KEY OF E

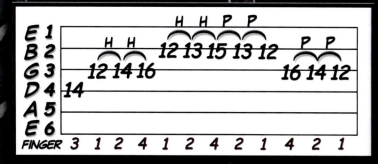
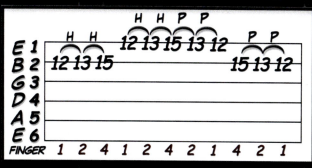

HARMONIC MINOR LICKS – KEY OF A

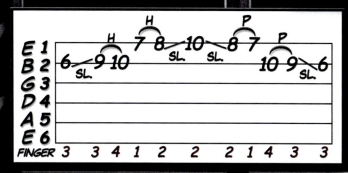
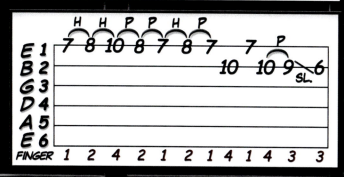

KEITH RICHARDS

KEITH RICHARDS WAS BORN ON DECEMBER 18, 1943 IN DARTFORD, KENT, ENGLAND.

KEITH'S GRANDFATHER WAS IN A JAZZ BAND THAT TOURED BRITAIN. HE WAS KEITH'S EARLIEST MUSICAL INFLUENCE AND GOT KEITH INTERESTED IN PLAYING GUITAR. (1953)

KEITH'S MOTHER BOUGHT HIM HIS FIRST GUITAR WHEN HE WAS 15. HE WOULD PLAY HIS GUITAR SITTING AT THE TOP OF THE STAIRS IN HIS HOUSE BECAUSE THAT IS WHERE THE SOUND WAS THE LOUDEST.

KEITH'S FIRST GUITAR HERO WAS SCOTTY MOORE WHO PLAYED IN ELVIS PRESLEY'S BAND. (1957)

KEITH SPENT MOST OF HIS TIME IN HIGH SCHOOL LEARNING TO PLAY GUITAR. KEITH AND HIS FRIENDS WOULD GO INTO EMPTY CLASSROOMS AND PLAY GUITAR FOR HOURS AND HOURS. (1958)

AFTER KEITH HEARD MUDDY WATERS, HOWLIN' WOLF, AND ESPECIALLY CHUCK BERRY PLAYING ELECTRIC GUITARS, HE TRADED SOME RECORDS FOR HIS FIRST ELECTRIC GUITAR, A HOLLOW-BODY HÖFNER. (1959)

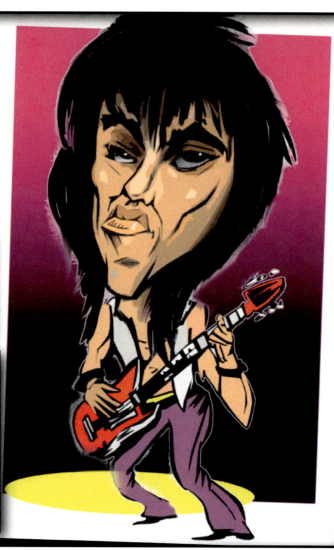

ONE MORNING ON THE WAY TO SCHOOL WHEN KEITH WAS 16 HE GOT ON THE SAME TRAIN CAR AS MICK JAGGER. (KEITH AND MICK HAD LIVED IN THE SAME NEIGHBORHOOD AND WENT TO THE SAME SCHOOL UNTIL KEITH'S FAMILY MOVED WHEN HE WAS 10 YEARS OLD.) THEY RECOGNIZED EACH OTHER AND TALKED ABOUT THE BLUES RECORDS MICK HAD WITH HIM. (1960)

MICK WAS SINGING IN A BAND AND INVITED KEITH TO A REHEARSAL. KEITH JOINED MICK'S BAND AND THEY MET BRIAN JONES AND IAN STEWART WHILE OUT PLAYING GIGS. TOGETHER THEY WENT ON TO FORM THE ROLLING STONES WHEN KEITH WAS 18. (1962)

KEITH WAS 20 YEARS OLD WHEN THE ROLLING STONES MADE THEIR FIRST ALBUM. (1964)

CHORD CONSTRUCTION

CHORDS START WITH THE **ROOT** NOTE AND THE **5TH**.

TRIADS ARE CREATED BY TAKING **EVERY 3RD** NOTE FROM THE **MAJOR SCALE** (C D EF G A BC). 1ST (ROOT), 3RD, 5TH.

ADD THE **NATURAL 3RD** AND YOU HAVE A **MAJOR** TRIAD.

ADD THE **FLATTED 3RD** AND YOU HAVE A **MINOR** TRIAD.

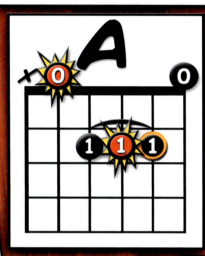

ROOT

MAJOR 3RD

MINOR 3RD

5TH

TIME TO LEARN SOME CHORDS!

AS YOU WILL SEE ON THE FOLLOWING PAGES ...

YOU CAN REPLACE THE 3RD OF A MAJOR OR MINOR TRIAD WITH THE 2ND OR THE 4TH TO CREATE "SUS" CHORDS.

YOU CAN ADD THE 9TH TO A TRIAD TO CREATE "ADD9" CHORDS. YOU CAN INCLUDE THE FLAT 7TH, THE MAJOR 9TH, THE SHARP 9TH, THE 11TH, ... ALL THE WAY UP TO THE 13TH.

COMPLEX CHORDS SOUND BEST WITH A CLEAN TONE. DISTORTION MAKES THEM SOUND VERY MESSY. (TURN DOWN THE GAIN.)

SUS CHORDS

"SUS" IS SHORT FOR "SUSPENDED." REPLACE THE 3RD OF A MAJOR OR MINOR TRIAD WITH ... THE 2ND OR THE 4TH

QUICKLY ALTERNATE BETWEEN THE REGULAR CHORD (MAJOR OR MINOR) AND THE SUSPENDED VERSION.

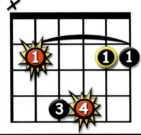
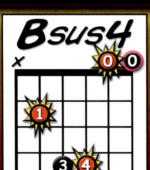
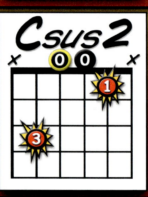

ADD9 CHORDS

● ADDING THE 9TH (THE 2ND TRANSPOSED UP ONE OCTAVE) TO THE BASIC TRIAD CREATES AN "ADD9" CHORD. THESE CHORDS SOUND COOL. SOME OF THEM ARE A STRETCH. BE PATIENT.

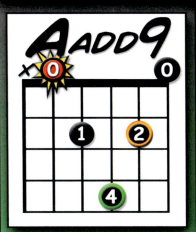

Aadd9

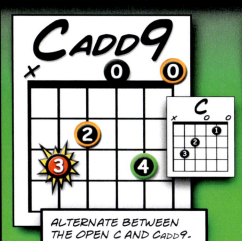

Cadd9

ALTERNATE BETWEEN THE OPEN C AND Cadd9.

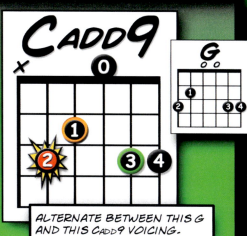

Cadd9 / G

ALTERNATE BETWEEN THIS G AND THIS Cadd9 VOICING.

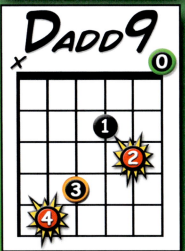

Dadd9

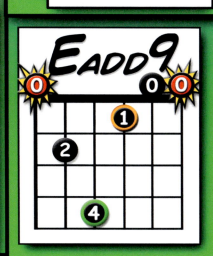

Eadd9

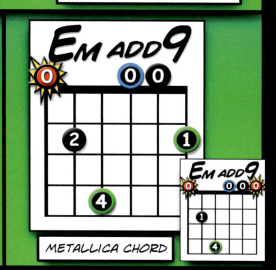

Em add9

METALLICA CHORD

Fadd9

1ST FRET: Fadd9
3RD FRET: Gadd9
5TH FRET: Aadd9
7TH FRET: Badd9
8TH FRET: Cadd9
10TH FRET: Dadd9
12TH FRET: Eadd9

Gadd9

53

7TH CHORDS

● ADD THE FLATTED 7TH TO THE BASIC MAJOR TRIADS TO CREATE "DOMINANT 7TH" CHORDS. 7TH CHORDS ARE POPULAR IN BLUES AND ROCK AS ALTERNATIVES TO TYPICAL CHORDS.

7TH BARRE CHORDS

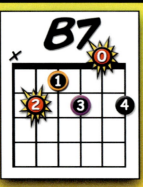

6TH STRING ROOT

1ST FRET: F7
3RD FRET: G7
5TH FRET: A7
7TH FRET: B7
8TH FRET: C7
10TH FRET: D7
12TH FRET: E7

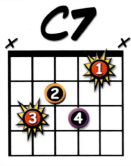

1ST FRET: C7
3RD FRET: D7
5TH FRET: E7
6TH FRET: F7
8TH FRET: G7
10TH FRET: A7
12TH FRET: B7

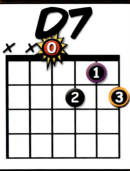

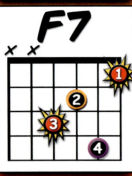

5TH STRING ROOT

2ND FRET: B7
3RD FRET: C7
5TH FRET: D7
7TH FRET: E7
8TH FRET: F7
10TH FRET: G7
12TH FRET: A7

MAJOR 3RD

54

Minor 7th's

ADD THE FLATTED 7TH TO THE MINOR TRIADS TO CREATE "MINOR 7TH" CHORDS.

MINOR 7THS

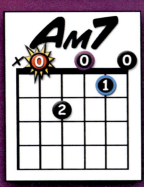
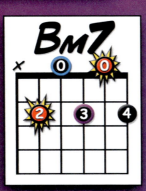
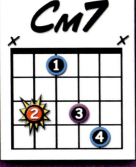
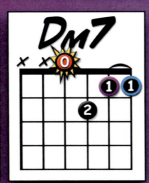
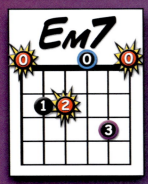
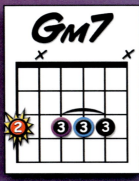

MINOR 7TH BARRE CHORDS

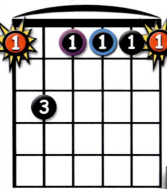

6TH STRING ROOT
- 1ST FRET: Fm7
- 3RD FRET: Gm7
- 5TH FRET: Am7
- 7TH FRET: Bm7
- 8TH FRET: Cm7
- 10TH FRET: Dm7
- 12TH FRET: Em7

7TH

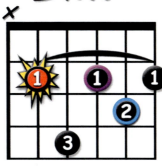

5TH STRING ROOT
- 2ND FRET: Bm7
- 3RD FRET: Cm7
- 5TH FRET: Dm7
- 7TH FRET: Em7
- 8TH FRET: Fm7
- 10TH FRET: Gm7
- 12TH FRET: Am7

MINOR 3RD

9TH CHORDS

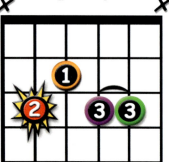

C9 — 5TH STRING ROOT

- 1ST FRET: B9
- 2ND FRET: C9
- 4TH FRET: D9
- 6TH FRET: E9
- 7TH FRET: F9
- 9TH FRET: G9
- 11TH FRET: A9

A PROPER 9TH CHORD IS A 7TH CHORD WITH THE 9TH (THE 2ND SCALE DEGREE ONE OCTAVE HIGHER) STACKED ON TOP.

THE 5TH CAN BE OMITTED.

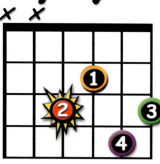

F9 — 4TH STRING ROOT

- 1ST FRET: E9
- 2ND FRET: F9
- 4TH FRET: G9
- 6TH FRET: A9
- 7TH FRET: B9
- 9TH FRET: C9
- 11TH FRET: D9

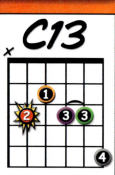

C13

GET FUNKY!!

ALTERNATE BETWEEN THE 9TH AND THE 13TH.

 9TH

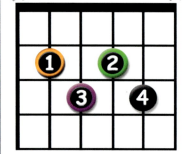

G9 — 6TH STRING ROOT

- 2ND FRET: G9
- 4TH FRET: A9
- 6TH FRET: B9
- 7TH FRET: C9
- 9TH FRET: D9
- 11TH FRET: E9
- 12TH FRET: F9

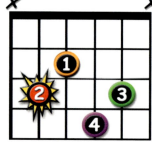

Cmaj9 — 5TH STRING ROOT

- 1ST FRET: Bmaj9
- 2ND FRET: Cmaj9
- 4TH FRET: Dmaj9
- 6TH FRET: Emaj9
- 7TH FRET: Fmaj9
- 9TH FRET: Gmaj9
- 11TH FRET: Amaj9

MAJOR 3RD

 C9 — 7, 8, 9, 10

ROOT NOTE

MINOR 9TH'S

Gm9

6TH STRING ROOT

1ST FRET: Fm9
3RD FRET: Gm9
5TH FRET: Am9
7TH FRET: Bm9
8TH FRET: Cm9
10TH FRET: Dm9
12TH FRET: Em9

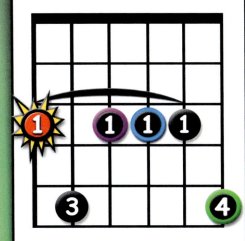

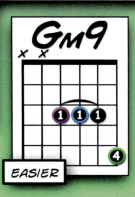

Gm9 (EASIER)

MINOR 3RD ●

Cm9

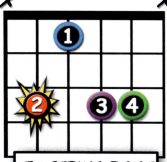

5TH STRING ROOT

1ST FRET: Cm9
3RD FRET: Dm9
5TH FRET: Em9
6TH FRET: Fm9
8TH FRET: Gm9
10TH FRET: Am9
12TH FRET: Bm9

THE "HENDRIX" CHORD

7TH ●

IF YOU ADD A **SHARP 9TH** YOU GET A "SEVEN SHARP-NINE" CHORD. IT IS GREAT FOR BLUES, ROCK, AND FUNK. JIMI HENDRIX USED THIS CHORD IN "PURPLE HAZE" AND "FOXY LADY."

C7#9

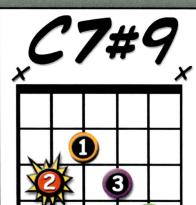

5TH STRING ROOT

1ST FRET: B7#9
2ND FRET: C7#9
4TH FRET: D7#9
6TH FRET: E7#9
7TH FRET: F7#9
9TH FRET: G7#9
11TH FRET: A7#9

E7#9

USE THE OPEN 6TH STRING WHEN PLAYING THE E7#9.

57

ELEVENTHS

ADD THE 11TH (THE 4TH SCALE DEGREE TRANSPOSED UP ONE OCTAVE) ON TOP. 11TH AND 13TH CHORDS ARE NOT VERY COMMON IN ROCK. YOU FIND THEM MORE IN JAZZ. IT IS GOOD TO KNOW WHAT THEY ARE AND WHAT THEY SOUND LIKE. (YOU HAVE TO ADMIT THEY SOUND PRETTY COOL!)

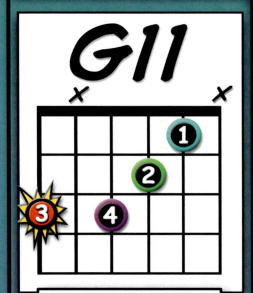

G11
6TH STRING ROOT
- 1ST FRET: G11
- 3RD FRET: A11
- 5TH FRET: B11
- 6TH FRET: C11
- 8TH FRET: D11
- 10TH FRET: E11
- 11TH FRET: F11

THE 5TH IS OMITTED

Gm11

MINOR 3RD

THE 9TH IS OMITTED

6TH STRING ROOT
- 1ST FRET: GM11
- 3RD FRET: AM11
- 5TH FRET: BM11
- 6TH FRET: CM11
- 8TH FRET: DM11
- 10TH FRET: EM11
- 11TH FRET: FM11

Gm11 — EASIER

Dm11

5TH STRING ROOT
- 1ST FRET: CM11
- 3RD FRET: DM11
- 5TH FRET: EM11
- 6TH FRET: FM11
- 8TH FRET: GM11
- 10TH FRET: AM11
- 12TH FRET: BM11

Dm11 — EASIER

13TH CHORDS

The 13th is the 6th scale degree one octave higher. 13th chords can technically contain all the notes in the scale, but some notes get left out since guitars don't have enough strings and we don't have enough fingers to play all 7 notes. The most important notes are the 3rd, 7th, and 13th. The 5ths, 9ths, and 11ths can be left out.

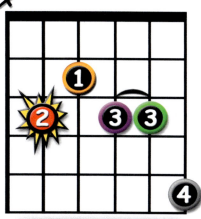

5TH STRING ROOT
- 1ST FRET: B13
- 2ND FRET: C13
- 4TH FRET: D13
- 6TH FRET: E13
- 7TH FRET: F13
- 9TH FRET: G13
- 11TH FRET: A13

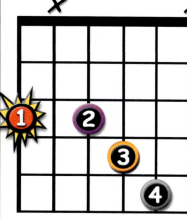

6TH STRING ROOT
- 1ST FRET: F13
- 3RD FRET: G13
- 5TH FRET: A13
- 7TH FRET: B13
- 8TH FRET: C13
- 10TH FRET: D13
- 12TH FRET: E13

MINOR 13TH CHORDS

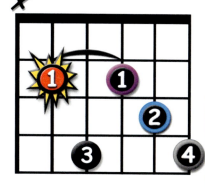

5TH STRING ROOT
- 2ND FRET: Bm13
- 3RD FRET: Cm13
- 5TH FRET: Dm13
- 7TH FRET: Em13
- 8TH FRET: Fm13
- 10TH FRET: Gm13
- 12TH FRET: Am13

EASIER

13TH

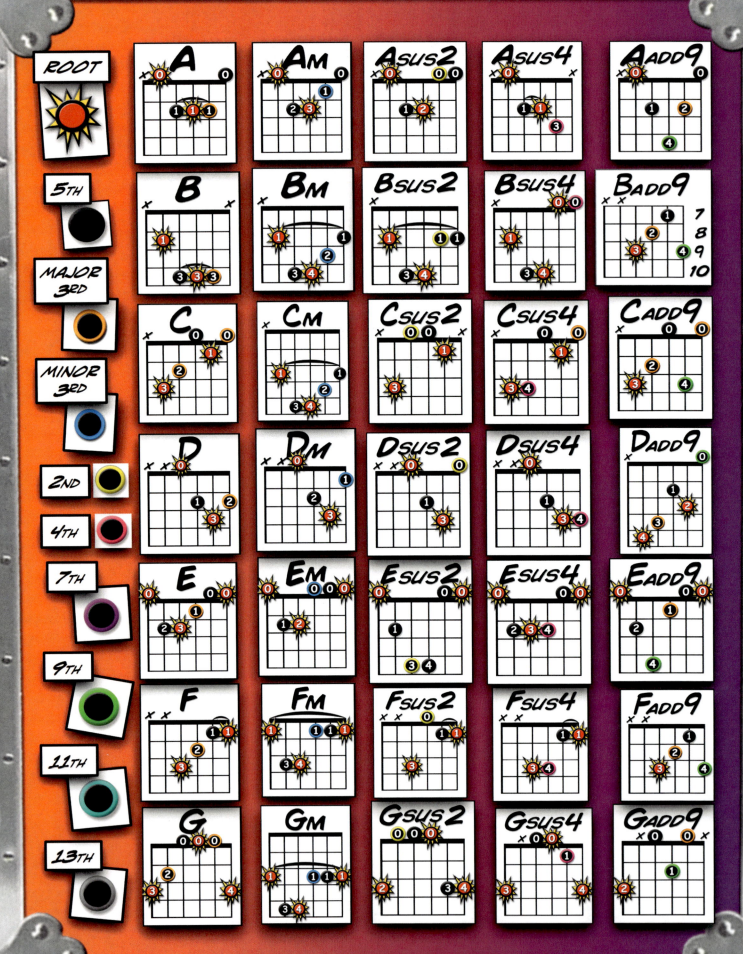

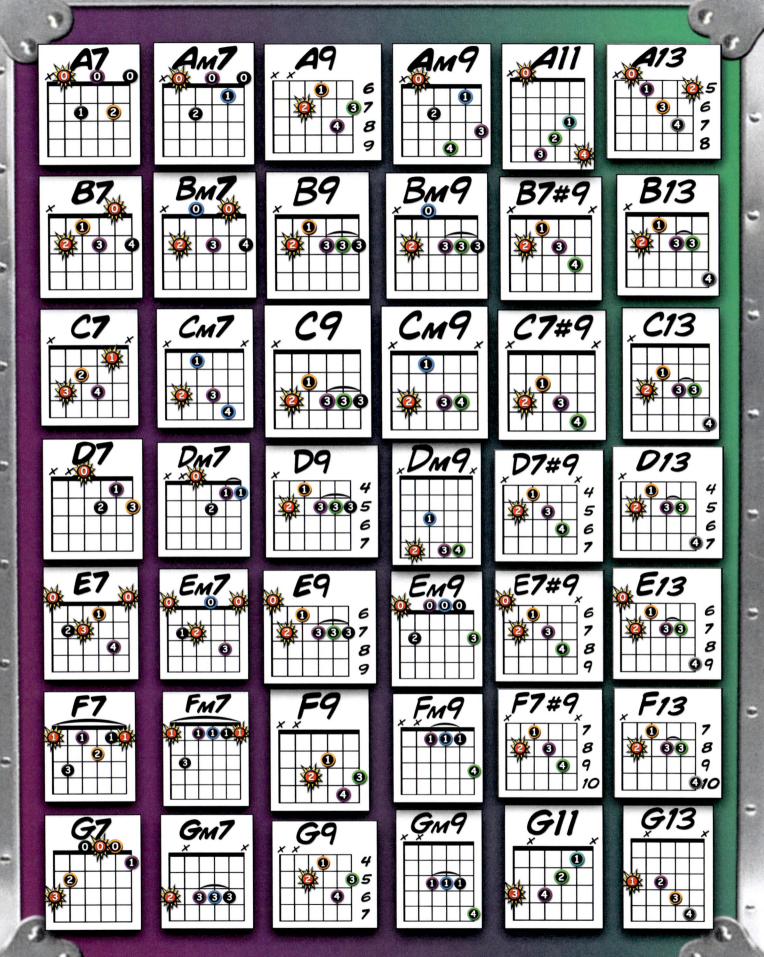

PICKUPS, AMPS, FX

YOUR CHOICE OF GUITAR, AMPLIFIER, AND EFFECTS DETERMINES THE TYPE OF TONE YOU ARE ABLE TO CREATE. DO YOU WANT A TIGHT, HEAVY, METALLIC TONE? A LOOSE, WARM CLASSIC ROCK TONE? A CLEAN, BLUESY TONE? FIND OUT WHAT KIND OF GUITAR, AMP, AND EFFECTS YOUR FAVORITE GUITARIST USES AND TRY TO GET A SET-UP THAT IS SIMILAR TO THEIRS. EVEN A BUDGET VERSION OF THEIR RIG WILL GET YOU CLOSE TO THE TONE YOU WANT.

PICKUPS

SINGLE COIL

PICKUPS PRODUCE A BRIGHT, CUTTING TONE RICH IN HIGHER HARMONICS. THE PROBLEM IS THEY CAN BE NOISY. THESE PICKUPS ARE COMMON IN FENDER STYLE GUITARS. JIMI HENDRIX AND STEVIE RAY VAUGHAN USED SINGLE COIL PICKUPS.

HUMBUCKER

PICKUPS PRODUCE A SMOOTH, ROUND TONE WITH A MORE POWERFUL SIGNAL AND MORE SUSTAIN THAN SINGLE COILS BUT WITH LESS NOTE DEFINITION AND HIGH END. THEY ARE NOT AS NOISY AS SINGLE COIL PICKUPS. HUMBUCKERS ARE COMMON IN GIBSON STYLE GUITARS. JIMMY PAGE, SLASH, AND EDDIE VAN HALEN USE HUMBUCKER PICKUPS.

AMPS

THERE ARE TWO TYPES OF AMPS - **TUBE AMPS** AND **SOLID-STATE AMPS**. MOST PROFESSIONAL GUITARISTS USE TUBE AMPS - THEY SOUND GREAT BUT THEY ARE EXPENSIVE (AND HEAVY). IF YOU ARE JUST GETTING STARTED GET A SOLID-STATE AMP THAT HAS A 12 INCH SPEAKER AND 30 TO 50 WATTS. YOU WILL BE ABLE TO PRACTICE WITH IT AT HOME AND YOU WILL BE ABLE TO JAM WITH A DRUMMER. IF YOU BUY A SMALL "PRACTICE" AMP WITH AN 8 OR 10 INCH SPEAKER YOU WILL NOT BE ABLE TO HEAR THE GUITAR OVER THE DRUMS.

EFFECTS

THERE ARE A FEW ESSENTIAL EFFECTS THAT EVERY GUITAR PLAYER SHOULD HAVE: A DISTORTION OR OVERDRIVE PEDAL, A WAH-WAH PEDAL, A DELAY PEDAL, AND A PHASER OR FLANGER PEDAL.

THINK OF EFFECTS AS SPICES WHEN YOU ARE COOKING ~ A LITTLE ENHANCES THE FLAVOR, TOO MUCH WILL RUIN IT.

TYPICALLY YOU WILL PUT YOUR EFFECTS IN THE FOLLOWING ORDER, BUT EXPERIMENT TO SEE WHAT WORKS BEST FOR YOU. (READ IT FROM RIGHT TO LEFT) ...

AMP < DELAY < CHORUS/FLANGER/PHASER < FUZZ/DISTORTION/OVERDRIVE < WAH < GUITAR

CHANGING YOUR STRINGS

AT SOME POINT YOU WILL NEED TO CHANGE THE STRINGS ON YOUR GUITAR - EITHER BECAUSE YOU BREAK A STRING OR THE STRINGS GET OLD AND GO "DEAD."

WHAT YOU WILL NEED:
1) NEW SET OF STRINGS
2) STRING WINDER
3) SMALL WIRE CUTTERS
4) ELECTRONIC TUNER

DON'T MAKE IT HARD FOR YOURSELF!
USE LIGHT GAUGE STRINGS. IT WILL BE MUCH EASIER WHILE YOU ARE DEVELOPING YOUR COORDINATION, STRENGTH, STAMINA, AND THE CALLUSES ON THE TIPS OF YOUR FINGERS. USE "-09'S" ON YOUR ELECTRIC GUITAR AND "-10'S" ON YOUR ACOUSTIC GUITAR. (DON'T WORRY, THE GUY AT THE GUITAR STORE WILL KNOW WHAT YOU ARE TALKING ABOUT.)

CAUTION: **ONLY REMOVE ONE STRING AT A TIME!** (AND DON'T POKE YOUR EYE!)
THE TENSION OF THE STRINGS CREATES A LOT OF PRESSURE ON THE NECK. RELIEVING ALL THIS PRESSURE AND THEN QUICKLY ADDING IT BACK CAN CAUSE SERIOUS PROBLEMS FOR YOUR GUITAR.

START BY LOOSENING THE STRING AND UNWINDING IT FROM THE TUNING PEG. TO REMOVE THE STRING FROM YOUR GUITAR, SNIP OFF THE BENT PART THAT WAS WRAPPED AROUND THE PEG.

STRETCH THOSE NEW STRINGS!

FEED THE NEW STRING THROUGH THE BRIDGE. BRING IT UP THE NECK AND SLIDE THE END OF THE STRING THROUGH THE HOLE IN THE TUNING PEG.

USE YOUR STRING WINDER TO TURN THE TUNER TO WIND THE NEW STRING. AS IT TIGHTENS BE SURE THE STRING IS SITTING PROPERLY ON THE BRIDGE OF THE GUITAR.

THE FIRST WINDING GOES ABOVE THE EXPOSED END OF THE STRING. THE REST OF THE WINDINGS GO UNDER THE EXPOSED END OF THE STRING. MAKE SURE THE STRING WRAPS NEATLY AROUND THE TUNING PEG.

TO CONTROL HOW THE STRING WRAPS AROUND THE TUNING PEG REMOVE THE SLACK BY CREATING TENSION. AS YOU WIND THE NEW STRING, USE YOUR OTHER HAND TO PULL THE STRING DOWN AGAINST THE FRETBOARD.

ONCE YOU'VE WRAPPED THE STRING AROUND THE TUNING PEG, BRING THE STRING CLOSE TO BEING IN TUNE. **SNIP OFF THE EXCESS STRING WITH YOUR WIRE CUTTERS.**

NEW STRINGS NEED TO BE STRETCHED. PULL EACH STRING ABOUT AN INCH AWAY FROM THE NECK. RE-TUNE THE STRING AND STRETCH IT AGAIN UNTIL THE STRING NO LONGER GOES OUT OF TUNE.

LIKE EVERYTHING ELSE, CHANGING YOUR STRINGS BECOMES EASY AFTER YOU'VE DONE IT A FEW TIMES.

Rock History 101

1930	**DELTA BLUES**	CHARLEY PATTON, SON HOUSE, LEAD BELLY, BUKKA WHITE
		NATIONAL RESONATOR GUITARS
1935		**ROBERT JOHNSON** — STELLA ACOUSTIC GUITARS
		RADIO AND 78 RPM PHONOGRAPH RECORDS
1940	**WORLD WAR II**	**THE GREAT MIGRATION FROM SOUTH TO NORTH**
		RAY CHARLES, FATS DOMINO, LOUIS JORDAN, T-BONE WALKER
1945	**RHYTHM & BLUES**	CHICAGO BLUES – **MUDDY WATERS**, HOWLIN' WOLF, ...
		THE 3 KINGS: B.-B.- KING, ALBERT KING, FREDDIE KING-
1950		FENDER TELECASTER GUITAR INVENTED. FENDER AMPS.
1955	**ROCK N' ROLL**	**ELVIS PRESLEY** — **CHUCK BERRY**
1957		LITTLE RICHARD, JERRY LEE LEWIS, BUDDY HOLLY, BILL HALEY, BO DIDDLEY,
1958		SUN RECORDS, FENDER STRATOCASTER GUITAR, AM RADIO & 45 RPM RECORDS
1962	**BOB DYLAN**	SONGWRITERS BECOME POETIC, PERSONAL, AND POLITICAL.
1963	**THE BEATLES**	**BRITISH INVASION** — **THE ROLLING STONES**
1965		THE YARDBIRDS, THE KINKS, THE WHO, THE ANIMALS ...
1967	**JIMI HENDRIX**	THE BYRDS, THE GRATEFUL DEAD, THE DOORS
		CREAM ~ ERIC CLAPTON — **GIBSON** GTRS. — **MARSHALL AMPLIFIERS**
1969	**LED ZEPPELIN**	
1970	**CLASSIC ROCK**	AEROSMITH, AC/DC, BLACK SABBATH, PINK FLOYD, BAD CO.
		DEEP PURPLE, THE FACES, HUMBLE PIE, THIN LIZZY, RUSH
		LYNYRD SKYNYRD, MONTROSE, KISS, CHEAP TRICK, ZZ TOP
1975		FM RADIO, 8-TRACK TAPES, AND LP RECORDS POPULAR
1977	**PUNK ROCK**	THE CLASH, SEX PISTOLS, THE RAMONES — **BOB MARLEY**
1978	**VAN HALEN**	**NEW WAVE OF BRITISH HEAVY METAL**
1980	**RANDY RHOADS**	JUDAS PRIEST, UFO, MOTÖRHEAD, IRON MAIDEN, DEF LEPPARD
1985	**THRASH METAL**	**METALLICA** — MEGADETH, SLAYER, ANTHRAX — **STEVIE RAY VAUGHAN**
1987	**SUNSET STRIP**	MÖTLEY CRÜE, RATT, POISON... — **GUNS N' ROSES** — MTV CD'S
1990	**GRUNGE**	**NIRVANA** — PEARL JAM, SOUNDGARDEN, ALICE IN CHAINS...
1995	**MODERN ROCK**	FOO FIGHTERS, RED HOT CHILI PEPPERS, GREEN DAY, ...
2000	**NU-METAL**	PANTERA, KORN, TOOL, RAGE AGAINST THE MACHINE ... MP3'S
2010		THE WHITE STRIPES, QUEENS OF THE STONE AGE, LAMB OF GOD, MASTODON, AVENGED SEVENFOLD ... IPOD'S
2015	**!!!!!! YOU ARE THE NEXT CHAPTER IN ROCK HISTORY !!!!!!**	

PERFORMANCE TIPS

PRACTICING YOUR CHORDS, SCALES, LICKS, AND RIFFS ALONE CAN GET BORING. JUST REMEMBER, YOU ARE PRACTICING FOR THE TIME WHEN YOU CAN GET TOGETHER WITH YOUR FRIENDS AND JAM. PLAYING MUSIC WITH YOUR FRIENDS IS SO MUCH FUN! EVEN MORE FUN IS PLAYING MUSIC WITH YOUR FRIENDS IN FRONT OF AN AUDIENCE!

IF YOU STEP ON THE STAGE YOU HAVE A RESPONSIBILITY TO THE AUDIENCE TO BE PREPARED AND DO YOUR BEST TO GIVE THEM A GREAT SHOW. THAT MEANS YOU USE ALL OF YOUR TALENT AND IMAGINATION TO ENGAGE AND ENTERTAIN YOUR AUDIENCE.

PRACTICE THE WAY YOU WANT TO PLAY. PRACTICE IN YOUR GARAGE THE SAME WAY YOU WANT TO PLAY ON STAGE. IF YOU PRACTICE WITH YOUR HEAD HANGING DOWN AND NOT MOVING YOUR FEET, THEN THAT IS THE WAY YOU WILL PLAY WHEN YOU ARE ON THE STAGE. PRETEND EVERY PRACTICE IS A DRESS REHEARSAL.

LEARN HOW TO PLAY STANDING UP. WHEN YOU PLAY A SHOW WITH YOUR BAND ARE YOU GOING TO BE SITTING DOWN?

LOOK AT THE AUDIENCE. EYE CONTACT WITH YOUR AUDIENCE IS VERY IMPORTANT.

AND WOULD IT KILL YOU TO SMILE A LITTLE BIT? GIVE A SMILE AND A NOD TO THE PEOPLE YOU KNOW IN THE AUDIENCE.

PLAYING ON STAGE CAN BE INTIMIDATING AT FIRST, BUT LIKE EVERYTHING ELSE WITH THE GUITAR, IT BECOMES EASIER AFTER YOU'VE DONE IT A FEW TIMES. PLAY ON STAGE AS OFTEN AS YOU CAN AND YOU WILL GET BETTER AND BETTER AT IT.

EDDIE VAN HALEN, JIMMY PAGE, SLASH, ANGUS YOUNG, AND ALL THE OTHER ROCK STARS LOOK TOTALLY AT HOME ON STAGE. THEY DIDN'T START OUT THAT WAY. **TO BE COMFORTABLE ON STAGE YOU NEED THE CONFIDENCE THAT ONLY COMES FROM EXPERIENCE.**

SEE AS MANY LIVE CONCERTS AS YOU CAN. WATCH VIDEOS OF YOUR FAVORITE BANDS TO SEE HOW THEY DO IT.

PRACTICE THE WAY YOU WANT TO PLAY!

DON'T ACT LIKE A ZOMBIE ON STAGE!

THE GREAT GUITAR PLAYERS...
- ~ PRACTICED ALL THE TIME WHEN THEY WERE YOUNG.
- ~ WERE PASSIONATE ABOUT PLAYING THE GUITAR.
- ~ PLAYED IN BANDS WHEN THEY WERE TEENAGERS.
- ~ WROTE ORIGINAL SONGS.
- ~ NEVER GOT DISCOURAGED.
- ~ RECORDED THEIR FIRST RECORDS WHEN THEY WERE IN THEIR EARLY 20'S.

LEARN AS MUCH AS YOU CAN FROM THE GREAT PLAYERS, BUT ALSO WORK TO DEVELOP YOUR OWN UNIQUE STYLE AND IDENTITY AS A GUITAR PLAYER.

LEARNING TO PLAY THE GUITAR REQUIRES **A LOT OF PRACTICE**. REPETITION CREATES...

MUSCLE MEMORY ... AFTER A WHILE YOUR MUSCLES WILL REMEMBER WHAT TO DO AND YOU WON'T HAVE TO THINK ABOUT IT. REPEAT THE SCALE PATTERNS AND LICKS OVER AND OVER WHEN YOU'RE WATCHING TV.

ROCK OUT!

TO IMPROVE YOUR TECHNIQUE ... *PRACTICE*.
TO IMPROVE YOUR EAR .... *LISTEN*.
TO IMPROVE YOUR MIND .... *STUDY*.
TO IMPROVE YOUR SOUL .... *LEARN*.

TO IMPROVE YOUR *MUSIC* ....
IMPROVE YOUR *TECHNIQUE, EAR, MIND,* AND *SOUL*.

GUIDE FOR PARENTS

THE SUCCESS OF YOUR FUTURE ROCK STAR LEARNING TO PLAY THE GUITAR DEPENDS ON YOUR ENCOURAGEMENT AND HELP. HERE ARE SOME TIPS TO HELP YOU HELP THEM ...

1. START WITH AN ELECTRIC GUITAR – ELECTRIC GUITARS ARE EASIER TO PLAY THAN ACOUSTIC GUITARS BECAUSE ELECTRIC GUITARS USE LIGHTER GAUGE STRINGS AND THE "ACTION" (HOW HIGH THE STRINGS ARE OFF THE NECK) IS LOWER. ELECTRIC GUITARS PRODUCE THE SOUND THE KID HEARS WHEN HE LISTENS TO HIS FAVORITE BANDS. IF HE WANTS TO PLAY ROCK OR METAL MUSIC, AN ACOUSTIC GUITAR SIMPLY WILL NOT PRODUCE THAT TONE. PLAYING ELECTRIC GUITAR IS EXCITING. IF HE'S EXCITED BY HIS GUITAR HE'LL BE MUCH MORE LIKELY TO PRACTICE AND STICK WITH IT.

2. GET AN AMP WITH A 12" SPEAKER AND AT LEAST 30 TO 50 WATTS – THEN THEY WILL BE ABLE TO PRACTICE WITH IT AT HOME AND EVENTUALLY THEY WILL BE ABLE TO USE IT TO JAM WITH A DRUMMER AND OTHER MUSICIANS. IF YOU BUY A SMALL "PRACTICE" AMP WITH AN 8 OR 10 INCH SPEAKER IT WILL NOT BE LOUD ENOUGH TO BE HEARD OVER DRUMS AND OTHER INSTRUMENTS. LOOK FOR AN AMP THAT HAS A HEADPHONE JACK WHICH MUTES THE SPEAKER AND ALLOWS THE PLAYER TO HEAR THEMSELF USING HEADPHONES WITHOUT DISTURBING OTHERS.

3. BUY THE BEST EQUIPMENT YOU CAN AFFORD – IT WILL BE EASIER TO PLAY, IT WILL SOUND BETTER, AND IF TAKEN CARE OF PROPERLY IT WILL LAST FOR YEARS AND RETAIN ITS VALUE. USED EQUIPMENT IS A GREAT WAY TO GET GOOD GEAR CHEAP.

4. FIND A GOOD GUITAR TEACHER – THIS IS CRITICAL TO THEIR DEVELOPMENT AS A MUSICIAN. MAKE SURE THE TEACHER WILL TEACH THEM WHAT THEY WANT TO LEARN. AGAIN, IF YOUR KID WANTS TO LEARN METALLICA, A TEACHER WHO IS NOT INTO METAL IS NOT GOING TO BE THE BEST FIT. IF YOUR KID IS HAPPY WITH THE TEACHER AND WHAT THE TEACHER IS TEACHING, THEY'LL BE MUCH MORE LIKELY TO HAVE FUN AND LEARN.

5. OFFER AN INCENTIVE – WHEN MY SON WAS 10 YEARS OLD I OFFERED TO BUY HIM A NEW ELECTRIC GUITAR WHEN HE COULD SHOW ME THAT HE HAD MASTERED EVERYTHING IN THIS BOOK. (IT DIDN'T TAKE LONG BEFORE I OWED HIM A NEW GUITAR!) OFFER TO BUY THEM A NEW GUITAR STRAP OR EFFECT PEDAL IF THEY LEARN TO PLAY A SONG ALL THE WAY THROUGH. (MAKE SURE THE GOAL IS ATTAINABLE.)

6. LET YOUR ROCK MONSTER CRANK IT UP! GIVE THEM 15 TO 30 MINUTES A DAY TO TURN UP THEIR AMP AND WAIL. THE AMPLIFIER IS MADE TO PLAY LOUD. IT SOUNDS BETTER LOUD. YOUR ROCK MONSTER NEEDS TO GET USED TO THE FEEL OF PLAYING AT LOUD VOLUMES TO PREPARE FOR THE TIME WHEN THEY CAN GET TOGETHER WITH A DRUMMER AND REALLY MAKE SOME NOISE! (P.S. BUY SOME EAR PLUGS!) **ENJOY!**

WWW.THEROCKMONSTERS.COM
COPYRIGHT© 2013

Made in the USA
Middletown, DE
15 December 2019